Hired for Youth

Fired for Age

Taking Charge of Your Career at 50+

REYNOLD LEWKE

Hired for Youth, Fired for Age
Reynold Lewke

be suitable for your situation. You should seek the services of a competent professional before beginning any of the programs and activities described in this book.

Throughout this book, trademarked names are referenced. Rather than using a trademark symbol with every occurrence of a trademark name, we state that we are using the names in an editorial fashion only and to the benefit of the trademark owner with no intention of infringement of trademark.

Published by Pecora Press
100 Pecora Way
Portola Valley, California 94028

Printed in the USA

ISBN13: 9780692509524 (Pecora Press)
ISBN 10: 0692509526

DEDICATION

To my beloved wife, who is a loving mother and
my best buddy, Laura Becker-Lewke—looking
forward to the next 60 years!

HIRED FOR YOUTH
FIRED FOR AGE

How understanding how the job market really works will help you overcome the implicit ageism in the system to take control of your career.

FOREWORD

Rich Karlgaard
Publisher, *Forbes Magazine*
Author of *The Soft Edge and Team Genius*

AMERICA IS DRIVING ITSELF CRAZY OVER EARLY achievement. My magazine, *Forbes*, celebrates young super-achievers in its annual 30 Under 30 issue, featuring today's crazy disrupters and tomorrow's brightest stars. *Forbes* isn't the only one to celebrate the precocious among us. *The New Yorker's* 20 Under 40, *Inc's* 35 Under 35, *Fortune's* 40 Under 40, and *Time's* 30 Under 30 issues spread the idea that if you haven't created a new industry or banked nine figures while still young enough to get carded, you've somehow wrecked your life.

This attitude of regret is unfortunate. Most of us—if we eat smartly, exercise, and confront our dysfunctional hobgoblins—have the potential to remain healthy and economically productive for another two decades past our retirement ages. Rather than regretting our past, we need to be embracing our future. It's not over at 60. Or 70. Or even 80. Never is it over. Now is the perfect time to cultivate our inner late bloomer and choose to remain vital.

Experience counts for something. So does conviction, perseverance, and grit. As we age and learn, our self-confidence increases, our planning abilities advance, and we readily seek new challenges. Our brain can handle these challenges. The latest research in neuroscience and cognition science shows how our brains remain plastic until near the end of our lives. This means, at any time, our aspirations and our sense of purpose can blossom. As Oleg Khazan wrote in a 2014 article in The Atlantic, "Genius, it seems, happens when a seasoned mind sees a problem with fresh eyes."

By that definition, Reynold Lewke, author of this book, is a true genius. His is a first-rate mind—seasoned by academic degrees in engineering, law and business from top universities, and a successful career placing C-suite executives in big jobs at global companies. When Reynold speaks about your career options, you can trust him. But the real genius of *Hired for Youth, Fired for Age* is how it goes beyond its practical professional advice. I love this book because Reynold encourages you to see with fresh eyes the big picture: Your finances. Your health. Your relationships. Your faith and moral compass. That's a lot to absorb in a book about second-half career options. But don't be daunted. Reynold Lewke is about to take you on an exciting—and doable—journey.

PREFACE

ARE YOU 50+ AND COMPLETELY HAPPY IN YOUR WORK, with a defined benefit pension and lifetime medical benefits secured? If so, this book is probably not for you. On the other hand, this book can help if you:

- ◆ Have concerns about the next 20+ years of your professional life,

- ◆ Are not sure what your longer-term career plans are or should be,

- ◆ Are confused by why search firms only occasionally call you and then rarely call back,

- ◆ Wonder if you've saved enough for a comfortable retirement,

- ◆ Wonder if you ever can or will be able to afford to retire, or

- ◆ Wonder how to find work that matches your skill sets, especially as you get older.

It is an old saying that the quality of your work life drives the quality of your life. A key to having good work-life quality is working at something that you enjoy, ideally something you would do for free. Identifying those opportunities that fit you well personally is dependent upon your knowledge of the job market.

The impetus to write this book has been borne out of seeing how poor job market knowledge has caused literally thousands of competent people to become frustrated in their professional lives, particularly after age 50. They often ultimately settle for something that does not really fit what they are capable of personally and professionally, nor does it correspond to what they would really like to do for themselves, their families, and society as a whole. The microeconomic result is great people who are under employed, under compensated, and not happy at work. The macroeconomic result is that immense amounts of highly qualified human capital are grossly wasted on a global basis.

This book has been 40+ years in the making, based on my years in executive search, engineering, legal practice, and business. By better understanding the realities of the job market, my hope is that you can create and implement a plan to make the next 30+ years personally and professionally fulfilling.

In reviewing thousands of career progressions, interviewing thousands of candidates, and hearing countless stories of how individuals are sometimes promoted, sometimes passed over, and sometimes fired, I have come to the conclusion that companies, and individuals, will state that they hire on the basis of some stated and perceived objective measures of competence:

Hired on Competence. To support that hypothesis and contention, they will point to multipage and detailed job specifications. What usually actually happens is that the specific manager simply hires another young person their own age who offers youthful energy, hipness, potential, etc.

However, when it comes time to fire, lay off, downsize, right size, or whatever the politically correct term then in vogue happens to be, the most common reason given is, "the individual just did not fit in with the team." Stated succinctly, they were Fired on Personality. Often, this personality or fit comment is another way of saying that the new younger manager no longer wants an older person, who distinctly reminds them of their parents, watching over them and possibly giving advice based on real experience. After all, this is the new world; there has been a "fundamental paradigm shift." It is all about "taking risks," and all that old thinking just slows things down.

If this has ever happened to you, this book will give you the tools to create a strategic career-life plan that will guide you to remain intellectually engaged in your work, while having a portfolio of income sources to make your "retirement" stimulating and financially rewarding. Understanding how to use these tools will enable you to be more thoughtful about selecting the environment in which you choose to apply your craft.

You are a unique set of talents and, planted in the right environment, will bloom and flourish.

Planted in the wrong pot, you will never achieve your full potential and may well wind up with either a shriveled root system or dead. With some additional tools in your toolbox, you can build and shape the next 30+ years of your life to be the best ever, and you can be a personal testimony of how experience and wisdom are at least equally important as youthful enthusiasm. Not only can old dogs learn new tricks, they can also teach some of the young pups some important lessons.

At the end of the day, success is based, as stated by the Romans long ago and that still rings true today, Per Aspera ad Astra, that is, Through Hard Work to the Stars.

Chapter One

WHY YOU NEED A CAREER-LIFE PLAN FOR THE NEXT 30 YEARS

*Things Have Changed Since
You Entered the Job Market*

IN THIS BOOK, WE WILL COVER:

1. The 3 reasons why you need to have a career-life plan for the next 30 years,

2. The 3 reasons why you rarely/never get a call back from a search firm and 3 steps to improving your odds,

3. The 5 steps to creating a meaningful strategic career-life plan for the next 30+ years of your life,

4. The 4 steps to implementing your career-life plan,

5. The 3 steps to staying professionally relevant until 2050, and

6. How paying it forward is your best career insurance policy.

The first question is, "Why do I need a 30-year career-life plan?" On its face, it seems that after working for 30+ years, people in their 50s should not be in a position to have to answer that particular question. As it turns out, there are numerous answers, factual, emotional, and spiritual, to that simple question. Let's start with, as Joe Friday made famous, "Just the facts, ma'am[1]."

Basic Overview of Current Financial Situation

As we begin, it is only fair to warn you that this first section contains a lot of data. These numbers are not meant to intimidate you. Rather, the purpose is to provide you with the basic information that you will need to make sound choices. So strap on your seatbelts and let's get going.

To begin, the US government, i.e., the Social Security Administration, believes that you, born sometime between 1955 and 1965, will probably be here in 2050[2]. Logic would then dictate that if you are going to be here in 30+ years, you should plan for it, rather than simply letting it arrive like an unexpected cold shower. According to an old adage, "Pity the man who plans to live to 90 and then lives to 95." Consider the alternatives. In the absence of planning, you're already there. Restated, **in the absence of planning appropriately, do you really want to be a PhD in astrophysics and working as a greeter at a big box store at age 78, trying to**

make ends meet? If that sounds a little dramatic, consider just some of the highlights of the current situation[3]:

◆ A 65-year-old couple retiring in 2012 was estimated to **need $240,000 to cover medical expenses throughout retirement**.

◆ Half of current retirees surveyed say they left the work force unexpectedly as a result of health problems, disability, or getting laid off.

◆ For a low earner retiring at 62, Social Security replaces 40% of pre-retirement earnings.

◆ Nearly 75% of retirees have not saved enough and said they would save more if they could do it all over again.

◆ More than one-third of all households end up with no employee-sponsored retirement plan at all during their entire work lives, and others, who move in and out of coverage, end up with inadequate 401(k) balances.

◆ At age 65 and above, Social Security benefits provide more income than any other source for over 60% of households, regardless of marital status. With an average monthly benefit of $1,330 for retired workers, this indicates that a lot of retirees are having challenges maintaining their standard of living.

♦ **One-third of households end up entirely dependent on Social Security; for low earners, that portion is 75%.**

♦ 60% of workers report that their total household savings and investments, excluding the value of their home and any defined benefit pension, is less than $25,000.

♦ 56% of workers report that they have not attempted to calculate how much money they will need to have saved for a comfortable retirement.

Even recent data shows that **average 401(k)/IRA balances reached only $91,300 in 2014**, with average balances almost $250,000 for people saving more than 10 years[4]. Using the traditional 4% rule, a rule of thumb typically used by financial planners to determine the safe amount of funds to withdraw from a retirement account each year, even the latter number for long-term savers only results in $10,000 annual income for retirement.

Reason 1: Changing demographics or, surprise, we are living longer than in the Good Old Days.

How did this happen? One of the big challenges facing baby boomers today is that since Social Security was created as part of the New Deal in 1935, life expectancy in the United States has moved from the early 50s to the mid-80s[5]. The "plan" was to work for "The Man" to age 65, get a nice pension for a few years, and then die in your 70s. In retrospect, something like that plan was probably the true basis for the assumptions on which Social Security was founded, because that was the way the world was when the legislation was drafted, and those were the typical expectations of most individuals.

In 1930, the US population was 123 million, with 49 million in the labor force, and 6.7 million ages 65+, and a mere 270,000 over 85[6]. That meant **over 7 workers per retiree**. **By 2010**, population in the US had grown to over 300 million, with 153 million in the labor force and over 40 million age 65+ and 5.5 million 85+[7]. That meant **3.8 workers per retiree**. **By 2050**, barely half of the 400 million people will be in the labor force, with 84 million over 65 and 18 million 85[8]+. With **barely over 2 workers per retiree**, the population age distribution that looked like a pointy pyramid at the time of the New Deal, and that was the basis for what some have described as the biggest government-sponsored Ponzi scheme in history, will by 2050 look like a soda can[9]. As everyone knows, if a pyramid scheme is not a pyramid, it collapses. Put another way, **there are already more people over 65 today than there were in the whole labor force when Social Security was passed**. By 2050, another 35 million will be over 65.

So the baby boomers all grew up with this idea in their heads that retiring at 65 was some sort of birthright and that the government would take care of things. But nobody planned on massive parts of the population living to age 80,

90, and beyond. The result of this constantly changing demographic for baby boomers was that, even as they were growing up, the ground kept moving under their feet, and the goalposts kept getting moved. Ironically, not only was this fact little advertised, but those who did were often shouted down in the clamor to preserve the political sanctity of Social Security. Clearly things have changed.

Reason 2: Corporate pensions are no longer your guarantee of retirement financial bliss.

Another factor that occurred during the first 30 years of your professional life since you entered the workforce is that the corporate pensions that were the mainstay of the generation that survived the Great Depression, World War II, and the buildup of the 50s and 60s, ran into the stagflation of the 70s, were systematically dismantled on the altar of Maximizing Shareholder Value by the Green Mail Raiders and Corporate Destroyers of the 80s and, therefore, became essentially extinct during the 1990s.

For example, when I started at United Technologies in the early 1980s, I attended a pre-retirement seminar. The HR department representative, then called Industrial Relations, explained that if I stayed with the company for 35 years, I would receive a pension that would be 50% of the last five years of employment before I retired at age 65. They continued with the statement that my living costs would go down by 50% when I retired because I would no longer have to commute to work, that my mortgage would be paid off, and thus I would be able to live at the same effective income level after retirement as I had been when I was working. This would be especially true, given that I would receive the bonus of Social Security in addition to my pension. At the time, I confess that I never thought to ask why magically 50% of my living costs would go down when I retired. In addition, no discussion occurred about what really impacts costs after age 65, such as the cost of prescription medications, medical costs, and other related costs.

In the classic shell game of the shareholder value champions of the 80s and 90s, these pensions were replaced with individual retirement accounts that were supposed to be even "better" than the old pensions. The 401(K) plans were supposed to take care of retirement needs by allowing individuals to decide how to invest in their own future. Again, the problem with assumptions is that they are only valid as long as they are valid. If the stock market goes up in a slow linear fashion, everything is fine. If volatility occurs and the values go up and down, then it all depends where on the graph you try to step off. Step off at the top and you look like a financial genius. **Step off at the bottom and you step off into poverty**.

What you think you can draw from savings is probably wrong.

Another implicit assumption was about the impact of what individuals would be able to draw from savings. **Scenario 1**: In that preretirement seminar held in the early 80s, at a time when inflation had been averaging above 10% since 1974, the expectation was that savings would increase 10% per year, so taking 5% per year would be a safe strategy for a 20-year retirement after age 65. Thus, the argument went, if you were a good thrifty citizen, after working 35 years for a major corporation, you would have investments and savings of at least $1 million. Five percent of $1 million is $50,000, combined with a 50% pension and $25,000 a year from Social Security, and your **retirement income would be comfortably well over $100,000 per year with "minimal living expenses."** The minimal living expenses part at the time was because most people would leave the snows of Connecticut to journey south to Florida for the warm weather and the lower cost of living.

Scenario 2: The math looks very different if you're talking about the "safe withdrawal percentage" of 4% of the $103,200 Median IRA balance[10], for the 55-64 age cohort, which equals $4,100 for the median IRA, no pension, and Social Security of $25,000 a year, for a **total of less than $30,000 per year**. One scenario has you traveling the world in retirement. The other has you in poverty or working at a fast food restaurant to cover medical expenses.

Briefly, to return to the initial question, why do you need to plan for the next 30 years? The brutally simple answer is that **in the absence of planning, you will wind up in scenario 2**.

Reason 3: Medical costs do not go to zero when you are 65+.

Another major assumption was the impact of medical costs as a portion of living expenses. Let's look at the generation that grew up with company health insurance plans that had begun in World War II. This insurance was a way of competing for labor in a time of strictly controlled wages, as a nontaxable fringe benefit, and it was generous, comprehensive, and cost essentially nothing. Therefore, for this generation, the concept of low-cost or no-cost medical care was again another birthright that extended into retirement. For the current generation of 50+ individuals, those golden company health plans are largely ancient history. Instead, even after the Affordable Care Act, perhaps a more aspirational title than factual, costs for the 50+ in the new world order are dramatically different than what was ever expected.

Once free plans covering everything, now even basic ACA plans now have $1,000+ monthly premiums and $10,000 per year deductibles in many urban parts of the country for working professionals[11]. If you want what you once had at your company, it will probably cost considerably more, perhaps twice as much. The biggest long-term challenge for individuals in this age group is that average increases in household income are barely above 2%, while health care costs are rising at 8%, so **by 2030, projections are that premiums and out-of-pocket costs will exceed $85,000 per year,**

which is the projected average US household income for 2030[12]. Clearly, while something will need to happen because logically people cannot spend everything they make on healthcare, it is also apparent that healthcare insurance and out-of-pocket expenses will be a major cost factor for individuals over the next 30 years.

Those are some of the facts that a thoughtful, mature professional needs to consider in the planning process that must occur if they are to take charge of their career as they paddle toward the increasingly turbulent rapids of the next 30 years.

If you consider those facts thoughtfully, directly, and as simply just another opportunity in your professional career, metaphorically, you will continue to paddle through the rapids, perhaps getting occasionally splashed from the spray and a little wet, but navigating successfully to calmer waters in the future. The alternative is to have no paddle and let your canoe get spun around in those rapids, flipped over, and then smashed against the rocks, with your physical, emotional, and financial well-being simply water-soaked pieces of flotsam in life's stream. Since the alternative is not altogether pleasant, let's examine some ways for you to remain master and commander.

Financial Basics 101 for the 50+ Crowd

Now, if you are slowly comfortable with the reality of needing to plan for at least 30 years, the question then becomes what are some of the cornerstones on which to base a plan. The first and most obvious are reasonable financial expectations with respect to things such as cost of living and sources of income. Ken Fisher, in his classic book, *Plan Your Prosperity*[13], deals with the issue of time horizon, which he succinctly states is longer than you think. For example, as he notes, if you take inflation as being 3% per year, which is its historical average, then if you need $50,000 per year today, admittedly, a rather minimal amount if you're living in any major city in the United States, that means that in 30 years you will need $120,000. **To match the 3% inflation rate, you need to have assets that are appreciating at least 7% per year so you can safely take out the recommended 4% of capital as your source of income**.

Alternatively, as Fisher points out, if you have been fortunate enough to **amass $1 million at age 55**, then 30 years later, it is worth just $400,000 in purchasing power. If you are taking out the prudent person's 4% annually, your effective buying power **draw has gone from $40,000 at age 55 to $16,000 at age 85**. So you really get whipsawed because your needs are increasing, while your draw is going down. Looking at it simply, if you need $50,000 at age 55 and are getting $40,000 from your savings and investments, you have a difference of $10,000 that needs to be made up somehow. At age 65, you need over $70,000, while receiving now just $32,000, so the delta has grown to $38,000. **By age 75, the shortfall has grown to over $70,000!** So just because you are part of the <1% of the population who has a $1 million portfolio at age 55, it does not mean you can just take the "safe" route, clip coupons, and expect that you will have anything resembling the lifestyle you thought you were setting yourself up for to still be comfortable at 85.

Having dealt with the issue of how inflation decimates your savings over time, Ken Fisher, in chapter 4 of *Plan Your Prosperity*[14], covers the reasons why the **classic rule, of take 100 minus your age** as being the percentage that you should have in stock, is **inappropriate for most professionals** today because of this 30+ year time horizon. These include that the time horizon is not how long until you plan to retire, but is rather how long you want your assets to work for you and for your spouse. As already discussed, since life expectancies, due to medical advances and nutrition, keep rising, and because often the spouse may be younger and healthier, the time horizon needs to account for all of those factors. In addition, the opportunity cost should be considered as the risk of doing nothing now may cheat you of superior returns down the road.[15]

News Flash! Guaranteed Lifetime Employment at Large Corporations Has Decreased

One of the fundamental realities that is changing is the importance of large corporations. While a tremendous amount of the world's economic power is concentrated in the 50 largest companies in the world, at the same time, over the last 50 years, there has been a shift in the number of individuals who no longer work for corporations, but rather work for themselves. This has sometimes been called entrepreneurism, but it is in many ways going back to what was the historical norm of where economic power lay or where goods and services were created. Traditionally, there was a guild system where young people came into a craft, such as shoemaking, and, as an apprentice, learned the basics for a number of years until they reached a certain level of expertise. They then set out as journeymen to travel to different places and explore with different masters variations on shoemaking. As these journeymen spent time understanding the differences in craftsmanship and materials from different parts of the country or different countries, they eventually became masters themselves and set up their own business. Then they would repeat the cycle by training apprentices and bringing in journeymen to expand their knowledge and receive the knowledge of other places and to stay current with new trends and technologies.

The US, like much of the world in the 18th, 19th and well into the 20th century, was dominated by industries that were essentially individual in nature, including agriculture, tradespeople, and various types of hands-on service providers and professionals. It was really the effect of World War I and World War II that caused the fundamental shift in the number of people who were engaged in small, often family-owned, businesses to large corporations. That needle has swung back from its peak in the 70s as a result of the economic shocks of the late 70s, 80s, 90s, and 2000's. Going forward, the trend will be for more individuals to become free agents. This concept was discussed in the book, *Free Agent Nation: The Future of Working for Yourself* by Daniel Pink[16]. He argued that much has changed since William Whyte wrote *The Organization Man* in 1956 and that instead of being captives of the organizational structures and strictures, income-earners are now free agents, including some 30+ million freelancers, temps, and micro-business owners. While the trend that Pink discussed has not developed as rapidly and as broadly as he had predicted, nevertheless, this trend to smaller, often single person, enterprises seems to be growing steadily in the US. The growth of large independent networks such as Facebook and especially LinkedIn underscore this trend to individuals having a voice they can communicate more broadly and the freedom to pursue new enterprises with relatively little investment risk.

Summary of Why You Need to Plan

To sum up then, the reason that you as a 50+-year-old professional need to really and thoughtfully plan the next 30+ years is that:

1. Your current financial plan and existing savings have a low probability of meeting your needs over that time horizon,

2. The realities of the consequences of your own and your significant other's life expectancy, and

3. The ever-increasing healthcare costs that flow from that longevity.

Taking charge of your life and career will require you to think about things probably somewhat differently than you have in the past, get brutally honest with yourself and the job market that exists today, and then develop and implement a process that will keep you professionally motivated with a high likelihood of personal satisfaction. With that in mind, let's move on to deal with some of the harsh realities of life, starting with the most puzzling of questions, "Why do I rarely/never get a call back from the search firm after they talk to me about some perfect dream job they are currently working on?"

Chapter Two

WHY YOU RARELY/NEVER GET A CALL BACK FROM THE SEARCH FIRM, ESPECIALLY AFTER 50

What Search Firms Never Tell You—
Either as the Client or the Candidate

ONE OF THE MOST FREQUENT QUESTIONS I AM ASKED BY well-qualified individuals is, "Why do I rarely/never get a call back from the search firm or from the company?" Given that the individual posing the question is often very academically and professionally accomplished, and would according to any normal objective measure seem to be an ideal candidate, the question is entirely fair. So let's explore why you rarely/never get a call back, especially as you pass 50.

What search firms rarely tell clients is that for most of the industry, a closing rate of <50% in six months is pretty typical.[17] Seen from the perspective of baseball, this is a pretty good average. Seen from the perspective of needing to find someone for a critical role in a timely fashion, this is often problematic and causes numerous side issues both during and after the search.

Why is the search process so long, so complex, and why does it so often lead to a less-than-perfect outcome? Several factors come into play, including the various personalities in the hiring company, the changing market conditions, the attractiveness of the company as a place to work, and the alternatives for well-qualified individuals. The result is a process that is long, drawn-out, and nonlinear.

A good example of a search not being successful the first time, and that this is something that can happen even to marquee companies such as Apple, occurred when the first successor to Ron Johnson, who left in November 2011, as Head of Retail, turned out to be an individual who lasted only a few months before being fired. A follow-up search for a successor lasted then many, many months, and it was an additional several months before that individual came on board in April 2014, for a total of over two years in process.

While the process is not always this long, and while there are a number of ways to make the process more streamlined and consistently successful, what follows is what happens in the "typical" search at the executive level.

What Really Happens in a Typical Search

To better understand why the process can be as difficult as it is, first let us consider a "typical search" for a VP of Sales at a "typical" midsize-to-large company. This is a company that has existed for a number of years, has well-developed human resource systems in place, including internal promotion and talent management systems, annual revenues in the hundreds of millions or even billions, and a corporate structure that has evolved over time to meet market conditions.

In this scenario, the search process starts one day when the VP of Sales walks in and unexpectedly tells the CEO that she is resigning to go to another company for more money and greater opportunity. After the initial disbelief, anger, frustration, etc., on the part of the CEO, and depending upon the CEO's mood that day, the VP of Sales is told to clean out her desk, hand over her laptop and cell phone, and depart the premises immediately or, if the CEO is feeling charitable, by the end of the day. After the now ex-VP of Sales leaves the building, the CEO picks up the phone, calls the head of Human Resources, explains what has just occurred, and tells her to find a new Sales VP as soon as possible.

What follows can most easily be understood by the following diagram:

Flowchart of a Typical Search

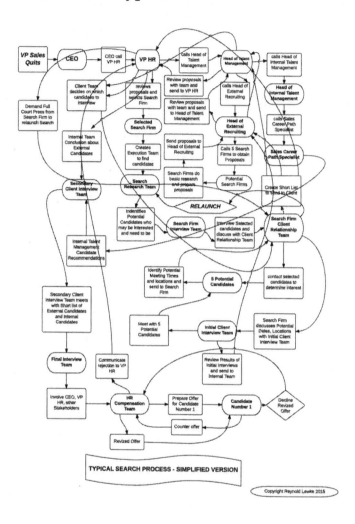

Now, some people might not immediately follow this simplified diagram of a search process. However, understanding this process is critical to your understanding of why you as a candidate rarely or almost never get a phone call back from the hiring company or from the search firm. In addition, if you do understand the process, you can make it work to your benefit by knowing how and when to interact with various search professionals.

The Need for Speed Arises

Let's unpack this process so it becomes perhaps a little clearer. Having received the call from the CEO, the VP HR alerts the head of Talent Management, that part of the Human Resources organization responsible for strategically meeting the human resource needs of the corporation. A well-run talent management organization considers both internal and external candidates and has a process in place that regularly reviews the current structure or corporation's bench strength, periodically tests external resources and benchmarks, and has a program for building executives from within the organization in a structured succession-planning model.

Internal Talent Management Process

So the Head of Talent Management alerts both the internal and external sources of supply for a new VP Sales. The internal talent management organization then swings into action by going from the head of internal talent management to the head of succession planning for the organization, and this individual then does an assessment of internal candidates who might be potentially available to fill the requirements of the VP Sales position. This involves reviewing and updating all of the performance appraisal reports of potential candidates and assessing whether those individuals who are considered high potentials, and have a potential successor in place, so they can be considered for a move into the new role.

Like a giant chess game, there may be some star candidate in the organization. However, if they are considered indispensable in their current role, which is often code language for the fact that their boss couldn't survive without the performance of that particular individual in their team, those stars are not available for consideration for this potential promotion as this would be considered damaging to the organization as a whole. As an aside, this star candidate will likely not take too kindly to the comment that they are considered indispensable in their current role and are, therefore, currently un-promotable. Handled poorly, this often causes those frozen stars to begin considering their options and may well trigger additional external search needs longer-term when those high potentials leave to unfreeze in a different company. In any event, to execute this whole process on the internal side often takes some weeks before an internal slate of potential candidates is available.

Starting the External Recruiting Side

Meanwhile, on the external side, the external-oriented talent management organization or recruiting group sends out a specification to typically five preferred search firm vendors and requests proposals from each of them. Since there has not been a VP Sales search in some time, and given that the job description for the departing VP Sales was crafted probably some five years previously and no longer matches what the CEO expects in the current environment, there will be a few days while the Talent Management organization, working with the appropriate parts of HR, crafts an appropriate specification that is appropriate for the new search. If the client is in a great deal of hurry, which is the normal state of affairs in such situations, they may send out the old spec to get the ball rolling, with the caveat that this will be revised before a final contract authorizing the search is signed.

Each of the bidding search firms then goes through the process of looking at the old spec, trying to guess potential changes to the spec, and then doing a preliminary database search to come up with an initial list of candidates that demonstrate to the client that the search firm understands the client's needs and, more importantly, has access to the appropriate level of qualified candidates and, therefore, should be the preferred vendor for this particular search. Since the spec is not finalized, there will be some questions back and forth between the research group preparing the proposal and doing the initial database run for candidates and the client interface team of the search firm, which includes the partner who has the relationship with that particular potential client. This client relationship partner, in turn, will then have discussions with their contacts in the client organization, trying to assess what might be the critical decision factors, all with an eye to crafting their proposal to be the most attractive.

A Search is Born

So how much time has passed to this point? From day one, when the outgoing VP Sales walked into the CEO's office and the CEO called the Head of HR, a handful of days will have occurred internally while a spec is created, reviewed, and approved, and then a few more days will pass in the interchange between the various search firms and the talent management organization. By the time the various proposals, amendments, questions, and other iterations have occurred so that a search firm is finally selected, typically two weeks will have passed since that first meeting in the CEO's office. This assumes that everything is going smoothly and there are no particular issues with respect to either the position, its location, or some background situation with the company. If any of these things occur, another week or two can easily pass before the selected search firm is under contract and starts to seriously scour the market.

Given the optimal efficiencies in this connected market, the research group now responsible within the research firm for identifying candidates will swing into action and begin their systematic sweep of the marketplace. The expectation on the client's part is to have the best, most qualified candidates and a reasonable selection. For many clients, that means they need to see at least seven or eight qualified candidates to believe that the search firm has done a proper job. On the search firm's side, it is not uncommon to reach out to 10 to 15 or more potential candidates for each short-list qualified candidate. That means that the search firm research team will reach out to and **speak to 80 to 100 potentially qualified candidates to arrive at the short list**. Even with a team of two or three researchers, this process will take one to two weeks, if everything goes well. If the spec is somewhat unusual, or requires something more challenging, such as the location is not in an ideal East Coast or West Coast location, this time can expand. In any event, if everything is going well, the time the VP Sales walked out the door to the time the first list of qualified candidates is presented to the client is often three to four weeks.

Logistics (and Stuff) Happens

Once the search firm sends out the rock star shortlist, the process switches over to the client side. The short list is reviewed by the client talent acquisition team, questions that arise are put to the search firm for clarification, comments on each are received from all members of the team, a ranking process occurs, and the results are sent back to the search firm for execution of the next step. Again, if everything goes smoothly, this review process can take two to five business days, depending upon the thoroughness of the discussions, the size and experience of the teams involved, the level of discussion occurring at this stage of examining and contrasting between internal and external candidates, the use of internal candidates as a benchmark against the external candidates, or vice versa, and just the travel schedule of the client team involved. After the review, the seven or eight proposed candidates will have been reduced to five top candidates for whom the search firm is told to arrange interviews. After all, for the client team to appear to be doing their job, some priorities will need to be set, so some potential candidates will be "voted off the island" at this phase.

Now comes the next level of complexity. Given that this is a national search for a reputable company, it is unlikely that all of the candidates are currently within a 30-minute drive of the client. Also, based on a variety of factors, an initial interviewing team on the part of the client must be decided and their schedules coordinated to identify appropriate 90-minute slots for interviews. If the typical internal team consists of just four individuals, then potentially ten travel schedules need to be harmonized to account for slots with respect to the five external candidates: the four internal interview team members and the search firm client coordinator who is part of the initial screening process. For sake of argument for this typical search, the client is located in Dallas, while the candidates are in New York, Los Angeles, Houston, Dallas, and Chicago. Since VP Sales candidates of the level that this client expects are generally visible in their own current companies and have demanding internal and external schedules, it is not unusual for three to four weeks to pass to be able to complete this first round of interviews with these first five top candidates.

The Empire Strikes Back, or Where are the Internal Candidates?

Once this first round has been completed, the internal talent management organization will now provide their input, recommending typically four internal candidates who should be seen as part of the process. To be thorough, these four candidates will need to be reviewed by the same team that interviewed the external candidates. Also, the internal candidates will be graded according to the same criteria set forth for the external candidates. Since they are internal, the client may more easily control the travel calendars of these individuals, so it should only take two weeks to review these internal candidates.

While the internal process is occurring, the search firm must continue to deal with the five candidates who went through the first round of interviews and also potentially keep warm the other two or three who were put on the back burner by the client. Typically, the leading two or three candidates will receive one call per week to keep them active, while the others will be told that contact will be reestablished as soon as the search firm gets a definitive answer from the client as to the next steps. Sometimes that callback occurs; sometimes it falls through the cracks.

Yet Another Round of Interviews

Now that the client initial interview team has seen the five external candidates and the four internal candidates, a ranking must occur to decide who will proceed to the next round. This next round will typically see three or four external and two or three internal to be interviewed by the secondary interview team, which likely includes the Head of Human Resources and the CEO. Again, given the realities of the schedules of the individuals involved, and because this involves the coordination of at least 10 to 12 travel schedules, another 3 to 4 weeks will pass before all of the candidates will have been seen by this interview team.

Keeping the Candidates Warm

Recapping the timeline, one month passed before the first slate of candidates was identified. A second month passed to interview the first round of external candidates. A third month passed to do the second round of external interviews and first round of internal interviews. Another week will pass while the client team assembles, reviews all the candidates, both internal and external, and creates a structured and thorough ranking. Based on that ranking, a decision will typically then be made to narrow the list from the external side to the top two candidates. Interestingly, if the reason for the search was unexpected, i.e., the VP Sales quit unexpectedly, there tends to be a bias on the part of clients to prefer the external candidates as being the source of "innovative new market-oriented insights." By now, almost three months have passed, and the CEO is anxious to get an impressive new VP Sales in place to keep the sales team motivated and headed in the right direction.

This ranking will be communicated to the search firm, and the request will be made to check references of the top two external candidates. Since this is a critically important position and the client does not want to take any chances, at least 10 references will need to be taken for each candidate. Since a good reference interview must be done either in person or on the phone and should typically last at least 45 to 60 minutes to properly cover any questions or issues and not simply be a rubber stamp, this process again will take approximately a week. After the results have been referred back to the client, there may be some follow-up if there are any potential caution flags that have been raised or additional concerns with respect to a particular candidate based on internal discussions of the client.

The Comp Committee Enters: Offer Negotiation Time

If everything is flowing smoothly, the go-ahead will then be given to refer the top candidate's compensation package to the corporate com-pensation and benefits group for creation of an offer to the top candidate. This will usually take two to three days, if everything is continuing like clockwork, and this compensation package will then be communicated to the search firm for presentation to the candidate. Actually, the top candidate, an outstanding sales professional, is well schooled in the art of negotiation and will not accept the initial offer and now comes back with a counterproposal. After the normal two days of consideration, after all this is a dating game, this counteroffer will be relayed back to the client and then processed by the compensation committee. There will follow another two to three days of deliberations, at which point the client will come back with their best and final offer. This will be relayed to the search firm to be discussed with the top candidate.

Client Offer is Rejected

However, by this point in many searches, it has now been almost four months since the search firm first contacted this particular top candidate about the position. With this much passage of time and now that some of the bloom may be off the rose, things may well have changed so much on the candidate's side, with some market changes, the timing of year-end bonuses may have become more interesting, etc., that after a week of negotiations back and forth, the top candidate ultimately declines the best and final offer from the client.

The rejection of the client offer will be passed along by the search firm client management team to the client. Frantic discussions will then occur, and given the length of time that has passed, the client will decide that market conditions are not what they were at the beginning of the search, expectations have changed, and the specifications have changed. With the passage of time, the number two top candidate is no longer deemed appropriate because they fail to meet the level set by the number one candidate. In turn, since only the best is good enough from the client's perspective, and there is now a need to find someone better than the candidate who turned down the offer, the bottom line decision is to relaunch the search with top priority so a new candidate can be hired within two weeks!

Relaunch Panic Time

As a result, the search firm research team goes back into action, now under enormous pressure to find interested candidates within the next four business days to give the client a sense of progress. This often involves going through another massive sweep of the market. However, if the research team did its job properly the first time, they have already talked to the top hundred candidates to get to that first shortlist. Going back after six months and telling well-qualified candidates that a job is still open raises questions in the minds of those candidates. That makes it more difficult to get top candidates interested in this now slowly-becoming-stale position. Like the real estate market when a house doesn't sell quickly, after time, even a good job gets tougher and tougher to sell.

However, since the VP Sales first walked into the CEO's office and said they were leaving, five or six months may have passed. Pressure from the CEO for a decision may well cause a reassessment of the internal candidates. In some cases, given the passage of time and a more realistic assessment of the attractiveness of the position to external candidates, a new internal candidate may be identified who, given the frustrations that the client has had with the external search process, will be put into the position so the organization can get some badly needed leadership after six+ months in limbo.

This does not mean that all searches end up in relaunch. However, given that the process deals with people and people are messy, the statistics show at least half will have a relaunch at some point in the process. This is the typical progress of a typical executive search for a typical company in today's marketplace. Remember, getting to the point of having a single external candidate to whom an offer was made took four months and required the search firm to contact probably almost 100 people. If you are one of the candidates who was engaged with by the search firm during that first month and did not make the short list of the initial seven or eight, the fact that the search firm did not speak to you for four months until after the top candidate declined the best and final offer from the client should not be a surprise.

Put another way, when you understand the process, you begin to understand why you rarely/almost never receive a call back, even if you are a remarkably well-qualified candidate who happened not to make the initial screen, for whatever reason. Thus, it is important to remember that receiving a call from a search firm about a great position that seems perfect for you rarely leads to an interview with the client or a job offer. The good news is that the search firm still has you actively in their databanks and is thinking of you. The bad news is that this is all that means. **Getting a call from a search firm does not mean getting a job offer**. Those who wait for such a call with the expectation of a job offer flowing automatically will wait a very long time.

How to Be a Helpful Backup Candidate

With an understanding of how the search process typically evolves, there are three steps you can take to increase your chance of being considered for this dream position and building your relationship with the search firm where they will actually call you back. The first thing to get clear on when you are talking with a recruiter for the first time is whether they are truly interested in you or really only want referrals, because, for whatever reason, they have already determined you are not an ideal candidate. If the recruiter has a laundry list of items that the client has indicated are must haves and you do not have, then you are not ideal. Trying to convince the recruiter that you are almost perfect is actually a waste of time for both of you. If they are sincerely interested in you, then you can take the conversation down that path.

The second step is that if they want referrals, you need to take your ego out of the situation, clearly understand what the recruiter is looking for, get a name, phone number, and email address, and promise to call back within 48 hours to discuss two good names. You then need to invest the time, research your contacts, and call back the recruiter with two qualified individuals they can contact. Ask the recruiter to let you know how it went.

The reasons for requesting a call back from the recruiter for feedback on your suggestions are that it allows you to see whether the recruiter, in fact, follows up on your suggestions and it indicates how professional they are. If they contact the individuals, and then get back to you, you have a reasonable opportunity to build a relationship. If they never call back, you can then put that recruiter on the unreliable list. Then if they do call back again another time, you could politely point out why you choose not to do business with them. For those who do call back, you can be a good source and build your bank of brownie points so when you need to call in a favor, you have a fighting chance of the recruiter and their firm being helpful.

The third step in keeping your options open on an interesting position is to periodically reach out to the search firm with recommendations for additional candidates. Thus, when the relatively frequent relaunch does occur, particularly if you were not selected and presented to the client the first time, you may be perceived as someone new in the market, you are top of mind to the search firm, you are clearly interested, and the chances are high that you will be flexible with respect to timing for interviews, thereby easing the process for the search firm. If the stars align properly, this might even be a way for you to get that job you are hoping for but were passed over on the first go around. Again, the client may also be more realistic with respect to expectations after having been turned down at least once, so your flexibility and qualifications may be more highly valued by the search firm and the client than they would have been in the initial beauty contest.

The big takeaway for you, a well-qualified professional, is that if a search that goes smoothly for an open position with a defined specification takes the best part of six months from kickoff, then **finding a new position where you are responsible for defining the need**, and so creating the position, is likely to take at least twice as long and **often takes 12 to 18 months**. That this is part of the reality of the job market is de facto recognized because most severance agreements at the executive level are for 12 months' salary continuance to cover this transition. So now that you understand why waiting for a phone call from a search firm as the basis for your next career move may not be where you put all the eggs in your basket, let's explore how you, understanding the need for a 30+-year plan, can take responsibility for that time horizon in the most effective way.

Staying Positive in the Desert

A key part of why you need to take this longer-term perspective and not become impatient is that you need to stay positive, upbeat, and proactive so when the opportunity comes, you are ready for it. The situation is analogous to the professional athlete who comes into a game off the bench and in the first 60 seconds of play, may well have the opportunity to turn the game around in favor of his or her team. If you are still pouting about the fact that you did not start, or were not presented in the first round of a search, you will not be at your best to give 100% effort when you have the opportunity.

Many years ago, I knew of an individual who had recently lost their job and was perfect from a skills perspective for the assignment of my search. The individual was excited and came to the interview with the client. When the client posed the typical question, "So what are you currently doing?," the candidate responded, "I am currently unemployed." The energy drop in the room was like air being let out of a balloon. Afterward, in discussing the candidates who had been presented, the client referred to this individual as someone who was still in the grieving process. The client did not have time for the individual to go through that on the client's time, as they needed someone to focus on the here and now in moving the company ahead.

The lesson learned is for you, irrespective of your position, to have the kind of positive mental outlook that communicates to a decision-maker who controls the potential opportunity that you are not only qualified technically, but have the mindset, energy, and enthusiasm of a true professional who wants to make a significant impact both in the near and long-term. Like the true professional soccer player coming off the bench in the 80th minute and scoring the winning goal two minutes later, no matter whether you start or are substituted in the last 10 minutes of the game, when you are on the pitch, you need to bring your top game. Goals in soccer, like opportunities in business, often turn on split-second timing and being able to seize good fortune. The true professional is mentally always prepared to be there and to be completely present in that moment and seize that opportunity. By having that mindset, the chances of being selected for those opportunities is increased, as are the chances that you will do a truly outstanding job should you ultimately be selected.

Summary of Why You Rarely/Never Get a Call Back

So let's recap why you rarely/never get a call back from search firms.

1. Even as the perfect candidate, you are one of 100.

2. Client companies have internal systems and logistics issues that can add a lot of time to the process.

3. Few clients have a perfect selection system to identify the best people from which to select.

4. Corporate compensation plans may not always be flexible enough to meet the ideal candidate's expectations.

5. The whole process takes so long that the search firm forgets about you in the changing mix of events.

The good news is that by understanding the process, you can improve your chances of being a better backup candidate. The even better news is that search firms really only handle about 10% of the market, with normal corporate postings worth about 10% of your time. The next chapter will discuss how you can create a process to tap into the 80% of the market that offers you the best opportunities for long-term, continued professional growth and opportunity.

Chapter Three

HOW TO CREATE A MEANINGFUL STRATEGIC CAREER-LIFE PLAN

Strategic Career Management Planning

TO GET FROM WHERE YOU ARE TO WHERE YOU WANT TO go most efficiently, most people would agree that you need a plan. The questions then become: what kind of a plan, how do you construct a plan, and what could be an appropriate plan? Since there is little reason to reinvent the wheel, the majority of large successful corporations that have been around for a while use some sort of strategic planning. If it has been working to keep IBM in its various iterations going for over 100 years, strategic planning might just be a useful model for how you go about thinking about your own life and career development over the next 30+ years.

Planning your career is really just a microcosm of the strategic planning process that most corporations have used for decades. Strategic planning is a tool that is been used by corporations to assess where they are, identify what they would like to become, and create a deliberate plan on how to get from where they are to where they would like to be. The word "corporation" comes from the Latin "corpus," which means a body of people or a body, and a corporation's purpose is to exercise the attributes of a person to create value. To be self-sustaining, that body must sell their products or services for more than what it costs to produce them. So, coming full circle, if corporations need to take a deliberate multiyear approach to achieving sustainable success, why should you, a mini corpus, take a different approach? So how do you apply a strategic planning to your professional career?

In this section, we will walk through an overview of the strategic planning process you can apply to your career and then delve into deeper discussions on various elements. In classic organizational strategic planning, you would start with what the entity stands for: vision, mission, and values. From there, you do the classic SWOT analysis: strengths, weaknesses, opportunities, and threats. This ultimately leads to major goals and specific objectives. How does this look for you as an individual? To begin with, you need to think about your **vision**: what you want to become; **mission**: what you want to achieve; and **values**: the standards of belief and behavior that are the basis for how you will live your vision and achieve your mission.

Step 1 - Creating the Vision Thing

If you have ever been part of a corporate strategic off-site to discuss these issues, you know that creating a vision and mission are not simple five-minute exercises. Nor do they necessarily stay the same over the years. These two items can have some variation over time as you evolve and explore what does and does not work for you.

Your values, on the other hand, need to remain the bedrock on which everything you do is built. Integrity is what you do when no one is looking. You may want to be a doctor and later a rocket scientist, but the values to live by to achieve those missions need to remain a firm foundation, or else when you get there, you may have lost everything.

Back to creating the vision thing. Classically, when you first came out of college, the career counselor probably asked you, "What do you want to be when you grow up?" This is something that can be very difficult to articulate because it is such a broad, open-ended question. You may need to think of a number of possibilities and brainstorm them with those closest to you. You may well need to write them down on a series of note cards that you can shuffle over a period of time before you come up with something that makes sense to you and that you can truly internalize. Also recognize, that over a period of years, this vision may evolve as a result of your life experiences. Remember that since you still have potentially 30 years ahead of you to develop in new ways, engaging in this process is still just as relevant as when you were coming out of college.

Clearly, with many years of experience under your belt, you have some good ideas about what you would like to become over the next 5, 10, 20, or 30+ years. Just be aware that you will want to revisit this question in five-year intervals to see how you're doing and whether it is still valid. The key to a good vision statement is that it is short, genuinely motivates you, and gets you excited to get up in the morning and charge forth to meet your destiny.

Step 2 - What is My Mission?

On to your mission: what do you want to accomplish, and how do you intend to accomplish that? As part of this process, you want to establish what is important, what has lesser value, what you wish to pursue, what you will leave for another day, and what the roadmap is for getting to that goal. This is where you need to set priorities and recognize that you can only accomplish one thing at a time. If you try to do everything at once, it will result in you doing nothing. With respect to vision, which establishes the grand goals for your life, the mission sets out how you concretely intend to get there.

Step 3 - What are My Values?

Finally, the issue of values. This is a topic that is as fundamental as breathing and is as much an issue of the heart as it is of the head. Writing this down is a useful exercise as it will be a baseline you can explicitly refer to for the principles by which you will abide in your personal and professional life. If explicitly written, you will be able to check yourself on it periodically and also show it to others so they can understand the basis for who you are. They, in turn, can act as accountability partners to help you stay on what can sometimes feel like a very narrow path, especially when you see "others" taking a seemingly easier route to achieve professional success. These values are the contract with yourself and with whatever Higher Power regulates the "big stuff" in your life. These are what David Brooks refers to as the eulogy virtues[18] and will be the ultimate legacy for which you are remembered.

Step 4 - SWOT Analysis

The SWOT analysis is all about trying to get a sense, in as complete and realistic a fashion as possible, of what constitutes your advantages and disadvantages. One of the challenging things that many professionals face is that it is often difficult on their own to assess their own strengths and weaknesses. When we look at ourselves in a mirror, we are actually seeing the reverse of ourselves. How others see us is, therefore, by definition, different.

This would be a good time to schedule a few sessions with some trusted advisors and spend some one-on-one time asking them how they see you. You need to go into this process with your ego firmly in check and be willing to hear some things that may be not altogether pleasant.

What you think of your strengths may not be what others perceive as your strengths. What you see as your weaknesses may not be how others see you. The reason this is important is because **it is others who will hire you for a position or as someone to work with, not you**. Thus, it is critical for you to understand others' perception of your true strengths and weaknesses.

This is not to absolve you of the need to do your own self-assessment. Stepping back from yourself, try to view yourself as objectively as possible so you can create a baseline for your own self-perception. In turn, you can use that image as a way to measure the input you receive from others. In so doing, as you go through the process now and periodically in the future, you will be able to continue to evolve processes tailored to you that will help you improve your strengths, eliminate or compensate for your weaknesses, and do it in a fashion that enhances your value to others most effectively.

STRENGTHS	OPPORTUNITIES
WEAKNESSES	THREATS

Thinking About Your Myers-Briggs Type

In doing your own self-assessment, this would be a useful time to think about reviewing your Myers-Briggs type[19] and the Johari window[20]. Like most professionals, while you probably have done these tests at some point in your career, now is a good time to review both of these mechanisms so you can use this updated information as a way of helping you establish how best to work with others. While there are a variety of online tests that discuss these models, the key is to take the results are with a reasonable grain of salt. Pragmatically think about what these tests might be telling you about how you perceive yourself, versus how others perceive you, and how you go about making decisions in your life.

Remember that these are tools to help you be more effective in the workplace and in your personal life and should not be considered straitjackets or absolute pronouncements on where your life is predestined to go or what you will become. Myers-Briggs is simply designed to measure how people perceive the world and make decisions. The Johari window helps remind you how your greatest strengths may be also the source of your greatest weaknesses, as they are the source of your blind spots. As Cassius so eloquently states in Shakespeare's *Julius Caesar*, "The fault, dear Brutus, is not in our stars, but in ourselves.[21]"

Hence, in addition to these tests, the usefulness of having others who you trust to be candid can help you identify those potential areas that, while seemingly to your advantage, could ultimately result in a serious misstep.

In discussing strength and weaknesses, particularly with your closest advisers, remember that strengths and weaknesses can originate from things that are internal to you, and over which you have some level of control, as well as from sources that are external and outside your ability to impact directly. Similarly, opportunities and threats have both internal and external components. In setting up a matrix that includes all four of these elements, be certain that you separate out those elements that are internal to you and those that are from external sources. To help keep yourself focused, it is best to use a series of bullet points so you keep your thoughts short and sweet.

The Process is Iterative

Take the time to go through this process thoroughly, and do not be afraid to go through a series of brainstorming sessions on each of these points. As you go through **the iterations, which may occur over a series of weeks or even months**, the things that do and don't work for you for the long term will become apparent. As you see the breadth of opportunities, the counterbalance of identifying potential threats provides a process for identifying those items that have the potential for seriously derailing your plans. When some inevitably arise, by working through those threat scenarios in advance, you will have a plan in place to deal with them. Rather than hurriedly scrambling to react, you will simply push the play button on your plan to deal with that potential problem. The idea is that threats are speed bumps, not sinkholes that swallow you up.

Having worked your way through the SWOT analysis, you can now create the goals and objectives that will make your vision and mission statements a reality. Your goals are the destination you wish to reach. They are an outgrowth of your vision. Your objectives are the steps you will take to achieve that goal. Once you articulate those goals and objectives, after investing so much time and energy in the process, an important part of being successful with this approach will be to periodically check and see what progress you are making.

In these **periodic evaluations, that can be every three months and at least annually**, you can take stock of what is and is not working and determine whether you need to make certain course corrections. Much of the time, these corrections will be minor, like adjusting the trim tab on the elevator to determine whether the airplane should be going up or down gradually. Occasionally, you will hit some severe turbulence, and you may need to take more active control and make more significant adjustments. However, with the over-arching goals and objectives in mind, any adjustments will be with the specific purpose of ultimately keeping you on track to achieve your vision.

Step 5 - How You Define Yourself

Using this career strategic planning process as a framework for analyzing how you want to properly plan the next 30+ years of your personal and professional life, you need to tackle a number of points that relate to who you are, your priorities, how do you define yourself, and your values.

As a start, do you define yourself by what you have accomplished, or do you define yourself by what others say about you? While those are often cited as being legitimate ways of thinking about yourself, each of them brings its own baggage. **If you define yourself by what you do, then when you are not doing something, who are you?**

In that regard, one of the most interesting comments I ever heard was from a guy who, after 25 years with a company, was required to retire at 65 and wasn't really happy with that decision. A few months later, he found himself at a networking event talking to a 20-something engineer. The young engineer asked the retiree, "So what you doing these days?" When the retiree responded with the phrase, "I'm retired," the young engineer asked, "So who did you use to be?" Ironically, that's the challenge for many people; and while this classically used to be a guy's problem, with the evolution over the last 30 years of the job market, this issue now confronts professional women, as well.

Special Challenges for Professional Women

Professional women face some unique challenges after the age of 50. Very often, they will have taken "some time off" to bear and raise children. They will also be looked to as the first point of contact when it comes to dealing with aging parents. As a society, these are important roles, and women, for a variety of biological and historical reasons, are cast in the role of having to do the "heavy lifting" in these areas. The problem is that the job market, driven by youthful gatekeepers, rarely recognizes these contributions, nor does it appreciate the skills of managing time and people that are implicit in these roles.

Professional women who left the workforce at some point in their career to perform these roles and later attempt to reenter the job market face the bewildering situation that the business world has moved so much (for example, in the area of technologies that are an integral part of the workplace and how business is conducted) that they may need in a sense to start all over again. Trying to reinvent yourself while trying to understand the new marketplace expectations and realities is a phenomenally difficult challenge.

You may well need to go back, in a sense, to your college days and look at your career choices as though for the first time. The marketplace reality is that you may be considered less desirable than your son or daughter who just graduated. As you look at the question of how you define yourself, you may need to consider a range of options, particularly in the near-term, that are "well below" where you should be given your track record, experience, and true skill sets. You may need to "descend the career ladder" from where you left off before you can re-commence your climb.

Defined by Accomplishments Trap

While defining yourself by what you have accomplished works because it is objectively clear what you have done, it contains a significant psychological trap. That is, if you are happy in whatever you happen to be doing, whether you are an engineer, interior designer, or lawyer, you are content. Conversely, if you are not currently content, this thought process of defining yourself by what you have done becomes a straitjacket that prevents you from honestly exploring your full potential because it is often very scary to venture outside of your comfort zone. There is a reason for the old saying, "Better the devil we know than the devil we don't know." Thus, this way of defining yourself by your accomplishments has some serious limitations.

Another common way of defining yourself is to get feedback about your strengths and weaknesses from others. Again, there are some advantages to this approach, as we discussed above, but it also some serious limitations. For example, how well does this approach work for you if you are in that group of individuals who are 50+, currently underemployed, between jobs, or just uncertain where they want to go next? If you are someone who is extroverted and draws energy and support from those around you, this approach may be legitimate if you are surrounded by "warm fuzzies" who are encouraging you.

If you are, however, like many technical individuals who happen to be of a more introverted nature and may not currently have a circle of friends who are empathically supportive, taking solely this approach can lead to some very negative views on self-worth and life. Even for extroverts, if things are not going so well in your company, with your friends, in your extended family, or in whatever ecosystem you happen to be a part of, defining yourself in this way can quite possibly lead to an evaporation of your sense of self-worth. Thus, in balance, this is a highly variable way of truly defining who you are and what will be the basis for your quality of life.

Nevertheless, understanding how others perceive you is a critical part of understanding yourself because it is critical for you to understand how the message you are trying to communicate is being interpreted. In summary, while this may not be the best way of defining who you are, it can still produce some very useful information for being able to interact with your environment and achieve your goals.

Stop Taking Things Personally

Following up on the challenging issue of how you define yourself, a significant cultural issue for many professionals in the United States and in many Western cultures is that we, as individuals, tend to take things personally. Once upon a time, boys were raised to be tough, show no fear, and never cry. Over the last few decades, the mantra has been for people to get in touch with their feelings and not to be afraid to show them. Ironically, this means that when we ask for a job and don't get it, we take it as a rejection of ourself as a person, rather than because the potential employer did not think we had the skill sets to do the job.

In ***Flawed System/Flawed Self: Job Searching and Unemployment Experiences***[22], Ofer Sharone discusses how different labor markets composed of individuals with very different attitudes can lead to a very different response to rejection. He goes into detail as to how the typical American desire to be in touch with one's feelings results in "chemistry games," where job seekers try to communicate to a potential job employer on the basis of some sort of values. He contrasts this with the Israeli market, where the perception is that success in finding a job is strictly based on how the job seeker performs on various tests, leading to a "spec games" mentality. He observes that the US worker, when rejected by a potential employer, tends to blame themselves and becomes depressed if this occurs time and time again. The Israeli worker, on the other hand, blames the system and not themselves. The result is that the Israeli job seeker finds it easier to stay emotionally positive about finding a job, rather than getting down on themselves for this constant stream of perceived personal rejection.

To deal with this tendency to take things personally, it is necessary to find an approach that allows you, the individual, to become more objective and strategic about what you bring to the job market and why someone should want to hire you to fulfill a certain role, build a product, or deliver a service.

One approach that has been effectively used over the years is to think of yourself as a product that you can identify with, so the discussion becomes not about you as the person, but about you as the product. Once you view yourself in the third person as some distinct, external, objective product, such as an automobile, analyzing this "You" product in classic terms of price, performance, etc., becomes emotionally and psychologically easier and allows you to achieve the necessary objectivity to understand how others perceive you in the marketplace. It also allows you to think about creating a marketing program for this product called You.

What is My Unique Selling Point—USP?

When building a marketing program about any product or service, one first needs to look at the features that make this product or service special. To be able to do that effectively, you need to look at the core components of that product, where it came from, what it is made of, how well it performs in different circumstances, and the best uses for the product. You need to take a thorough look at those aspects of the product so you can create the best possible marketing plan.

Accepting that others often see you simply as a product or service, just another widget, may be challenging at first for many people because, in one very fundamental sense, it attacks our core sense of identity and humanity. We often hear the phrase, "You are a person, not just a number or thing." Ironically, in today's modern business world, the real attitude toward people who work in an organization is reflected by the title of that part of the organization that is responsible for the care and feeding of the workers, typically called Human Resources. Some companies are moving to a Chief People Officer, rather than Chief Human Resources Officer, but the reality for most large companies or even midsize companies is that people are a fungible commodity, a resource.

According to an old saying, "You are irreplaceable until one week after you are dead." This may sound somewhat harsh, but it is the modern job-market reality. Once you come to terms with it, recognizing the shallowness of the sentiment that underlays this approach, you will not use your job title as a basis for defining your core identity and who you are as a person.

Taking Personal Inventory

With respect to that core sense of identity, it is good to take advantage of the fact that you once upon a time had dreams and aspirations, which have now in the interim been leavened by some 30+ years of career experience. The advantage that you have over the new hire coming straight out of college is that you have had experience in seeing what works and what doesn't work. The point is to take advantage of this experience to your benefit. However, since you are in essence at the midpoint of your 60-year professional career, let's take an inventory of where you have been and where you are now.

This is a good time to go back to that list you made in college, or may have made from time to time, about the things you wanted to accomplish, you wanted to learn, and more important, who you wanted to become. This inventory of who you are includes not only the usual degrees and titles, but also those skills you have discovered over the last 30 years in your professional career that you enjoy doing, can do really well, and can do perhaps better than most people you know. As you go through your personal inventory of likes and dislikes and reflect on your professional and personal life, those elements that make you special, i.e., your USP, should become apparent.

It is Not Real Until You Write It Down

Going through this exercise of articulating and writing down those skill sets that make you unique is critical, because only in writing it down does it become real. As long as you just have it in your mind, vaguely discussed from time to time with friends and family, it is not truly real. The Greeks of antiquity already understood that the word, once spoken, and particularly once written, has a life of its own.

This Logos has energy and a force of its own. Thus, the expression "sticks and stones may break my bones but words will never hurt me" is patently wrong. Words often can hurt and fester in ways that a physical blow never can. Your body can deal with the pain of an injury relatively quickly. The pain of rejection or a sense of failure can gnaw at the core of a person for decades and cause massive damage to the individual's sense of self, ability to relate to others, and even the ability to truly enjoy life. PTSD can originate from many different traumatic sources, and its impact should be respected.

Back to the list you have assembled that helps you identify where you are, the question then becomes where you want to go. Ideally, going through this process of examining what you enjoy, what you are good at, or what gives you energy will lead you to insights that allow you to determine some of the possible roads you might want to take. Determining the options requires serious self-reflection about what has worked, as well as what has not worked. It is important for you to understand that you learn from history so you do not repeat the mistakes of history, but like FDR, recognize that "the only thing [you] have to fear is fear itself.[23]"

To help with the process of identifying what should be your Big Hairy Audacious Goals, the BHAGs that are the core of many strategic planning sessions, think about what is really important at this point in your life. The midpoint of a career is a good time to contemplate what the vector of the next 30 years should be. What should be the guiding principles for that journey? What should be the North Star on which you set your compass, as you will inevitably encounter the waves and vicissitudes of a turbulent life? No one ever promised you a rose garden, and your life experiences have undoubtedly shown that there is no "free lunch." While you might want life to be "up and to the right," life needs to be recognized for all of its ups and downs and, therefore, a guiding principle that centers you on that journey is critically important.

Resume Virtues and Eulogy Virtues

Thinking about this issue, David Brooks discussed it in terms of resume virtues and eulogy virtues. As way to help you brainstorm and contemplate this next part of your life, it is useful to review his comments on this issue:

> *[R]ésumé virtues are the skills you bring to the marketplace. The eulogy virtues are the ones that are talked about at your funeral ...*
>
> *We all know that the eulogy virtues are more important than the résumé ones. But our culture and our educational systems spend more time teaching the skills and strategies you need for career success than the qualities you need to radiate that sort of inner light...*
>
> *But if you live for external achievement, years pass and the*

deepest parts of you go unexplored and unstructured.[24].

At this midpoint in your career, you have likely seen the realities of David Brooks' words. You have been down this road for the last 30 years and have seen the toll that it has taken on you and your friends. The question becomes: do I want to keep on doing this for the rest of my life? Insanity is often defined as continuing to do the same thing and expecting a different outcome. If you genuinely believe that there are aspects of your life with which you are not satisfied, and that you believe could and should be changed, then it is worthwhile thinking about the next 30 years as having a different focus. Now is a good time to think about what you want the next 30 years to be like and what you want to live for. Will it be the resume virtues, or will it be the eulogy virtues? Again, David Brooks provides some useful ideas and suggests perhaps a subtly different focus, that of the "stumbler:"

Commencement speakers are always telling young people to follow their passions. Be true to yourself. This is a vision of life that begins with self and ends with self. But people on the road to inner light do not find their vocations by asking, what do I want from life? They ask, what is life asking of me? HOW CAN I MATCH MY INTRINSIC TALENT WITH ONE OF THE WORLD'S DEEP NEEDS? ...

They are not really living for happiness, as it is conventionally defined. They see life as a moral drama and feel fulfilled only when they are enmeshed in a struggle on behalf of some ideal.

This is a philosophy for stumblers.
...

The stumbler doesn't build her life by being better than others, but by being better than she used to be[25].

Brainstorming Questions to Get You Started

If David Brooks' words resonate with you and you would like to look back on a life where you wore out rather than rusted out, you need to examine what you see as your particular resume virtues and eulogy virtues. To help get you brainstorming on this issue, consider the following questions as a starting point:

◆ What are you most proud of having accomplished?

◆ What dreams have you not been able to accomplish?

◆ If you did not have to earn a living, where would you spend your time?

◆ What aspects of your life, family, friends, personal activities, etc., are most important to you?

◆ When you graduated high school, what were your priorities?

◆ When you graduated college, what were your priorities and aspirations?

◆ What did you like about your first job, and why did you choose it?

◆ Why did you decide to leave your first job, including what attracted you to your new job?

◆ What were your priorities at age 30?

◆ What were your priorities at age 40?

◆ What were your priorities at age 50?

◆ What are your current priorities?

◆ Are you content with how things are going now?

◆ What concerns give you restless days or nights?

◆ Where do you go or to whom do you turn to receive affirmation of who you are?

◆ Thirty years from now, what will you be talking about with friends and family?

◆ Thirty years from now, what will you be most proud of having accomplished in that time?

◆ What things do you want to accomplish in the next five years?

◆ What things do you want to accomplish in the next 10 years?

◆ What things do you want to accomplish in the next 20 years?

◆ Who do you really want to be in the next 30 years?

This brainstorming, which admittedly centers on the question of values, is also a critical part of helping you identify and articulate your vision for your life, particularly the next 30+ years, and helping you develop your mission for your life. Similarly, it helps shape your own internal discussion on goals and objectives.

If You are a Tree, How are Your Roots and Branches Doing?

As a way to build on the ideas articulated by Brooks, in thinking how to go about determining who you are, a useful image is to think of yourself as a tree. The tree has numerous branches. These branches include work, health, family, friends, hobbies, volunteer work, and aspirational dreams. If these branches are growing in a balanced fashion, the tree continues to grow upward and flourish in a balanced way. If one branch becomes excessively long and heavy, the tree will start to lean in that direction, causing all the other branches to bend in somewhat unnatural ways and potentially causing the trunk to lean in the direction of the overly large branch. Thus, the tree will no longer be straight.

The trunk represents your core values and includes your sense of identity, faith, integrity, and other eulogy virtues. A strong and sturdy trunk can keep the tree growing upward, even if one of the branches is growing too quickly and attempting to shift the center of gravity of the tree in a different direction. However, if the branches are not kept in proper relation for an extended time, even these core values may ultimately suffer and bend in that direction.

Continuing the analogy, the issue is to ask yourself what is really driving you, or what is the source of your sustenance, including physical, spiritual, and mental? Where are those root systems going to reach out and draw in the energy and nutrients necessary to flow through the root system, up the trunk, and into the branches and leaves that allow the tree to grow? Making sure the tree is planted in proper soil, fertilized appropriately, and given the proper care and feeding and watering will result in a tree that continues to grow.

The question to pose to yourself regularly is, "Where are you getting your source of energy?" Where are you getting the energy to get up in the morning and go out into the day to be productive in all aspects of your life? Who are the people and what are the activities that give you energy? By contrast, who are the people and what are the activities that are energy draining? Trees planted in poor soil, that are improperly cared for, and even placed in the wrong size of pot will lead to the stunting and ultimate death of the tree. As you consider the next 30 years of your life, is it your desire to grow a giant oak, or are you focused on a small shrub?

These are some fundamental questions only you can answer. In addition, these questions are never simply asked once in your lifetime. Instead, they will need to be posed again and again on a periodic cycle, whether it is five years or at other natural breakpoints, because they often change at different stages of your life. It is unreasonable to suppose that what kept you truly focused as a college student will be the same as when you are shifting careers at 30 or taking on bold new challenges when you are 40, 50, and beyond. The important thing is to look at them thoughtfully, honestly, and directly and then identify what makes sense for you in the near term, as well as for you personally in the long term.

Building Core Strength

Following up on our earlier example of thinking of your life as a tree, you need to develop some core framework that will provide you with the basis for dealing with the challenges that you will confront over the next 30+ years.

Why is something that basic that important? The answer is that you need to have a way of dealing with the sheer frustration and boredom that at times will be a part of identifying and achieving the next step in your career path. Think about it: **if this process of finding the great next step for you will likely take 12 to 18 months, how do you keep your head in the game** and not get totally psyched out, frustrated, and otherwise disheartened in the process?

Job hunting and career management are often akin to the way bush pilots describe flying as hours and hours of sheer boredom interspersed with moments of sheer terror. How you deal with those moments of terror, such as a tough interview for an opportunity you would really like, is heavily dependent on how much your head is in the game at that moment. Like a corner kick coming to you in the dying moments of the championship game when the score is tied, will you jump high, see the goal wide, the keeper small, and drive it in for the winning score? Or will your jump be half–hearted, resulting in the ball bouncing harmlessly off your head to an opposing player? Being present at those critical moments will make all the difference in the trajectory that your life will take from that point forward. To achieve the best from those moments, you need to be prepared and ready to shine in that instant.

To be ready for those instances, you need to be in control at all times. Now, controlling something as dynamic as your life is at least as difficult as maintaining the positive dynamic stability of an aircraft. To achieve that level of control over a rapidly moving system, whether it is yourself or a high-speed combat aircraft, requires that you have control systems that are able to keep you going in the desired direction, at the appropriate altitude, and at the appropriate speed, notwithstanding environ-mental forces such as wind and weather, or potentially adverse enemy action where someone is shooting at you. First-order effects, such as encountering heavy turbulence and hail in a thunderstorm, can have very damaging consequences. Higher-order effects, such as the turbulence caused by air flowing over cities when you are at an altitude of 30,000 feet, have negligible impact. The point is that first-order effects can throw you off your equilibrium, while fourth-order effects are simply speed bumps.

In this area of control of your life, one of the great advantages about having been in the workforce for many years is that you have had a chance to try some things and see what does and does not work, or restated, what you can and cannot control. The other side of that coin is that you have had many years to develop some bad habits. If one of your goals in reading this book is to set yourself up for success for the next 30-plus years, you need to confront what is and is not working. There is little reason to change what is working well. What is not working well can be thought of, bluntly, as some sort of quasi-addictive behavior that is keeping you from achieving your goals and what you are capable of achieving.

The Circles in Your Life

To that end, one of the most successful programs over the last 70+ years can be grouped into what are known as twelve-step programs. At the core of these programs is a recognition that there are things that are bigger than you and the only way to truly get past them is to recognize your powerlessness over whatever it is that is holding you back and that you can only accomplish it through some force or Higher Power, often known as God, in whatever sense you understand it, as being the entity that can help change that. By recognizing that you are not in charge, that you need to rely on a Higher

Power and others who are willing to support you, you have a chance of making the changes in your life that will ultimately lead to a level of success and happiness that you previously have not experienced.

So recognizing that there is something bigger than you, that you are not an island unto yourself able to do whatever you please, whenever you please, and that Desiderata's admonition to "Go placidly amid the noise and the haste, and ... therefore be at peace with God, whatever you conceive Him to be,[26]" is something that should be number one in your life. Whatever impacts you in your relationship with that Higher Power is a first-order effect.

Circles of Personal Impact

Fundamentally, you need to recognize the reality of the concentric circles of personal impact in your life. The next circle is your life partner, your spouse, or whoever it is that shares your life on a daily basis. The care and feeding of that circle is a second-order effect and one that, should it go awry, will disturb you in a significant way. Thus, looking after the relationship of those closest to you is critically important to maintaining your focus and your ability to be effective in the workplace.

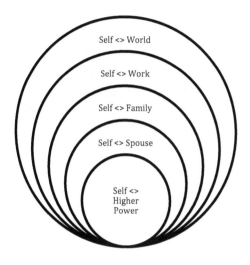

The next circle includes those in our nuclear family, typically children, parents, and siblings, with whom we have shared much, with whom we would like to share more, and whose love, respect, and admiration we truly value. If activities occur in this circle, it is a third-order effect. This is still important, but it is less important than the first two circles. Having a disagreement with your children, an argument with your brother, or an awkward Thanksgiving dinner with your parents should not be something that causes you to deviate from your intended life purpose.

The next circle is your work. This work–life balance is a fourth-order effect. What that means is that you need to hold yourself to the highest professional standards in the execution of your work, but understand that what happens in the workplace should not impact the first three circles of importance. **If things go awry at work, including getting fired, this is not something that should cause you to question your purpose in life, the love of your spouse and family, and the value that you have as a human being**. Work is important, work is something that you should do well, but work should not be "the tail that wags the dog" in your sense of who you are and why you were put in this world.

In his book, **When the Game is Over, It All Goes Back in the Box**[27], John Ortberg makes a point to recognize what he learned from his grandmother—if your life has its priorities confused, so that your work becomes the all-consuming addiction in your life and, therefore, your sense of identity, nevertheless, when the game is over, it all goes back in the "box." Win or lose the work-life game, it still all just goes back in the box. So maybe you should consider a different strategy, such as focusing more on eulogy virtues, rather than resume accomplishments.

What this circle of personal impact discussion should invoke in you is recognizing and valuing what is truly important for the long term. You may, at times, need to be like the onion and shed some of the outer layers and be willing to have some of those scuffed off. In contrast, your core values, and those most important to you, should always be held closest to your heart, for they determine who you really are. If you maintain your heart values, the other things in life will settle into their proper order.

Mindfulness in Career Management

Over the last few years, there has been increasing interest and discussion of mindfulness. It is important to understand that you need to take care of yourself, physically, emotionally, and spiritually, so you can maintain a sense of equilibrium as you encounter various adventures in your life. If you cannot take care of yourself, you cannot take care of others. There is a reason that airline safety briefings tell you to put on your mask first before helping others. Common sense tells you that if you are collapsing from lack of oxygen, it is difficult to help others.

Being mindful of your health means that you are able to work with your spouse and partner to have a positive impact on the world around you, whether it is raising children, dealing with aging parents, or helping your friends. From a social or workplace environment, if you are sick, you are absent.

Let's review what's important. If something happens to you, that is a first-order effect. If something happens to your spouse or partner, that is a second-order effect. If something happens to your extended family or close friends, that is a third-order effect. **If something happens at work, that is a fourth-order effect and should be treated as such**. Learning that lesson well will prevent you from letting a bad day at the office cause you to express yourself in road rage and, upon arriving at home, kiss your pet and kick your spouse. Staying in equilibrium, recognizing what is truly important in your life, will cause you to have a more meaningful and fulfilling personal and professional life.

Career Portfolio Theory

One way to think of your career is that it is similar to your investments. If the portfolio theory of investing is designed to maximize returns while reducing risk, then having a portfolio of multiple streams of income only makes sense for the long term. As you think of yourself more objectively as a series of skills, it is appropriate to think of applying those skills in a manner similar to your finances. In other words, if having a portfolio approach to your investments is what all the pundits tell you, why not apply that to how you think of your skills? If you think of yourself as a portfolio of income-generating opportunities, you can allow yourself to explore a greater variety of areas where you would like to apply your talents.

Why take this approach? For the same reason you do for your investments. As the old expression goes, you never put all your eggs in one basket. As individuals who worked at Enron discovered, having all your 401(k) consist of Enron stock was not diversification and had, for thousands of people, a catastrophic result. Particularly as you pass age 50, the need for a portfolio approach is increasingly important to support having a total income stream that meets current and expected financial commitments. Using the investment portfolio analogy, if small cap stocks are up and large cap stocks are down, then with a combination of the two in your portfolio, the wild swings in your portfolio are tempered. Similarly, if you look at applying your skills in several areas, then if one of those streams of income is reduced, you still have some options.

At the risk of stating the obvious that you have come to understand during the course of your professional career, another facet of this process is that nothing is permanent and everything changes. This means that trying to plan for 30 years in one go is likely to be as successful as the traditional multi-year plans were in Soviet Russia under Stalin and China under Chairman Mao. Rather, you need to think about six cycles of five years. Stated another way, you have six more chances, at least, to start and do something meaningful for at least five years. Each of these five-year cycles is an opportunity to reinvent yourself. Each five-year mission is a chance to go where no one has gone before, as Star Trek so aptly states.[28]

With the knowledge that you have multiple chances to create something completely new and special, it should also give you peace from knowing that you rarely have to worry that this is your only chance to do something. So then the question arises, what do you want to do?

Within the context of your vision, what might your near-term objectives be? This means that you should remain, to the extent possible, flexible as to where your desired career requirements take you. In this way, you are more likely to achieve your aspirational goals, such as enough income to pay the rent, combined with your long-term vision of creating a charity to support a beloved cause. Being flexible may mean that you should be open to considering something as radical as a change in location as a way to find the path to achieving your goals.

Rich Karlgaard, in **Life 2.0**[29], set forth in barnstorming style, à la "The Great Waldo Pepper[30]", to explore the US and meet with real people who found a sense of professional rebirth and a level of job satisfaction and contentment by changing the "**where of their happiness.**" This means that as you go through the process of pursuing your vision and achieving your objectives, you should remain open to serendipity that may steer you in a completely unexpected way to achieving your vision in a way that you had not previously considered.

Building Your Balance Sheet
So You Can Have an Income Statement

With the passage of time in your professional life, hopefully, has come knowledge. From knowledge, comes power. And as we all know from Spiderman, paraphrasing the Bible, with great power comes great responsibility[31]. The great responsibility you have is to invest yourself wisely. I use the term "invest" deliberately because it is important to think about your skills, and your life, as having both a balance sheet and an income statement. They are times when you invest and build up the balance sheet. Classically, that was the education and job training that you acquired early on in your career, typically in your 20s, which form the basis for being able to derive income. Sometimes, due to economic pressures, one has to sell some of the investments to generate cash and income. However, for the long term, it is important to have a sound balance sheet.

To that end, as you examine each day, think about how you are helping to continue to strengthen your balance sheet by acquiring new knowledge and new skills. Given the human brain's plasticity, you truly are never too old to learn anything. The instant your self-talk starts with, "I'm too old to ..," you are rapidly on your way to building a tombstone that reads, "Born year one, died year two, and buried year three." Lifetime learning is a way to build the balance sheet continuously and stay constantly relevant. So commit yourself each day to at least try to be learning something new.

With a strong balance sheet, you are in a position to absorb economic perturbations in a far better fashion. With a weak balance sheet, you are at the mercies of the economy and short-term blips. You are no longer paddling your canoe down the river of life; you are in a canoe without a paddle and entering the rapids. With a good canoe and a strong paddle, you can negotiate the rapids, and, while you may get a little wet from time to time, your canoe will successfully ride out the exciting times to enjoy the more placid pools that lay beyond.

Time for a Reboot?

Sometimes, it may be necessary to step back in one of the five-year cycles and say, "It's time to do a reboot." It is time to take a respite and go back to school. It is time to do something that focuses strictly on building the balance sheet. This can include going back to school full time or it can involve identifying a skill set that you need professionally, or wish to do personally, and invest yourself and your internal balance sheet. **Remember, if you are 50+ and considering the next 30 years, in a sense, you are exactly where you were when you were 20 and considering the next 30 years**. The advantage is that this time around you have a better sense of who you are, what works for you, and what is really important to you.

If you are wondering what some of the options can be, I recommend reading notes from your college class and seeing what your classmates are up to. You may be surprised to discover that some have gone back to law school or medical school or decided to become craftsmen in pottery, carpentry, or painting. Some may have decided to join a service organization and move to a new part of the country or even a new country as a way to repot himself or herself, trim off some of the branches, and settle into a new and larger pot that allows new roots to grow. Be open to the yearnings of your heart.

Summary of Strategic Career Planning

To recap this section, by thinking about your career and your life in terms of a strategic planning process, you have the framework on which to build the key elements of your life. These include:

- ✓ Identifying who you are
- ✓ What you want to become/achieve
- ✓ The values you stand for
- ✓ How you make your vision/mission a reality, and
- ✓ How you implement through concrete goals and objectives.

Next let's make this strategic career plan become reality.

Chapter Four

HOW TO IMPLEMENT YOUR STRATEGIC CAREER-LIFE PLAN

How to Get Where You Want to Go—Making Your Plan a Reality

HAVING INVESTED THE TIME TO CREATE A PERSONAL strategic career plan, how do you implement and make that plan a reality? What do you need to do to make your dreams a reality? The answer is well known and often cited. Thomas Edison was famously quoted as saying, "Genius is one percent inspiration and 99% perspiration." A variation on that is, "I now know over 1,000 ways not to make a light bulb." Whichever version you prefer, the truth underlying that statement is that very few things in life come about with the stroke of a fairy godmother's wand or a call from the lottery commission that your ticket is the winner.

The reality of implementing a dream is a lot of hard work. There is no way of sugarcoating this.

There is no way of wishing it away. There is no way of pretending that somehow you are different than everyone else in this particular regard. You cannot run a marathon by watching one on TV.

So what is involved in this process? Being 50+, you know and have experienced the realities of ageism. Now, to be fair, the generation that grew up in the 60s chanting at Woodstock to trust no one over 30 should not be surprised when their children or potentially grandchildren, who are the decision-makers or gatekeepers for a job, now express the same sentiment. At the risk of stating the obvious, the chance of someone under 30 giving you at 50+ a job is small. There are numerous reasons for this, not the least of which is probably the subconscious desire not to have parental supervision over their own career.

Oftentimes, the 50+ person finds themselves at a point in life where they need in some fashion to begin again and are psychologically looking at entering the job market for the first time, again. The challenge is that the techniques and advice that are rolling around in their head are now 30 years older than the last time they put together a resume and applied for a job.

Clearly, since 30 years have gone by, something must have changed. With the transparency of the Internet, the reality is that anything that is a published position receives numerous offers, often from completely unqualified people. The response to this carpet bombing by resume mills is for the screening function in the organization, whether internal to a company or external at some search firm, to try to automate the process, often through some computer program, and weed out resumes as quickly as possible in an automated fashion. The old saying that resumes get a 15-second scan by some new hire in HR is now down to fractions of a second by an OCR machine.

The byproduct of this mindless automation, from the perspective of the 50+ individual, is that your skills, like the baby, get thrown out with the proverbial bathwater. Professional women re-entering the job market after having taken time out for raising a family or caring for aging parents are especially liable to be knocked out by this automated process.

Step 1 - Building a Network that Actually Helps You

Who will take a chance on you; who will see your life experience as a positive and not as a negative? Who will recognize that just because you are over 30, you are nevertheless not yet brain-dead? The answers to these fundamental questions are, of course, someone your own age. Youth may be wasted on the young, but experience has learned to value experience. Therefore, if Wille Sutton's theory of banking was robbing banks because that's where the money was, you need to identify people who can identify with you. Simply put, you need to build a network of people who know you well enough and trust you so they will recommend you to others and, if able, offer you a job.

Building a network that supports you, particularly if this is not something you have worked on for a number of years or have not worked on from a professional sense, **is going to take time and a lot of effort on your part.** As a way to get you brainstorming on this process, here are some questions that should help stimulate your little grey cells to contemplate how to build a supportive network.

1. What networks, professionally and personally, do you currently have?

2. How do you feel about networks?

3. What have you invested in your professional networks?

4. What have you invested in your personal networks?

5. What professional networks would you like to develop?

6. What personal networks would you like to develop?

7. Who knows you best?

8. Who trusts you?

9. Who would take a chance on you to do something you think you can do but have never done before?

10. Who would you take a chance on to do something they have never done before?

11. Who are the bosses you most enjoyed, and where are they today?

12. Who are the coworkers you most enjoyed, and where are they today?

13. Amongst your friends and acquaintance, who are most successful in your eyes?

14. Which friends and acquaintances you have asked for help from in the past, and how have they responded?

15. Where are your classmates from high school, college, or graduate school?

16. Do you have a Christmas or holiday greeting card list? When was the last time you had a meaningful conversation with someone on that list, aside from sending the annual card?

To begin with, when you think about who knows you best and who would trust you enough to give you a chance to do something new, the classic response is your Christmas/holiday card list. The reason for this is that this list represents a group of people who have known you for a number of years and know you as a person. They have likely known you through a variety of seasons and have the greatest likelihood of being able to identify with your situation from a number of perspectives, not the least of which is that they know you, like you, and trust you. With this group, you have shared your own and your family's highs and lows over the years. You are a real person, not just a Facebook Like.

Step 2 - Building the Super Resume

Another part of the process in creating a network is to think about creating what can be termed a "super resume." This document, purely for internal consumption, should list essentially everyone you enjoyed working with, all of the coworkers you respected, all of the bosses who motivated you, and all of the people you managed and mentored over the years. It should include at least one highlight from every year of your professional life and should list any and all internal or external awards that you received and, ideally, why you received them.

Going back to your college days, you should also think about listing those individuals who had a significant positive impact on you, whether they were other students, administration, or professors. Who are some of the colleagues you collaborated with during your time in school? What extracurriculars were key parts of your life in college, irrespective of whether it was varsity basketball, intramural ice hockey, or the ballroom dance elective? Who were the key people you resonated with in those activities? Moving through the years, try to remember and write down individuals with whom you had strong positive interactions, whether in your personal life or in your professional life. Finally, do not forget all the parents of the children on the different sports teams that you have assisted while coaching, driving to games, or providing after-game snacks. This would also be a good time to pull out your yearbooks from high school and college and take a look at where your classmates, including those in your class, as well as those a year or two ahead of or behind you, are today.

The purpose for creating this super resume is to get you thinking about how broad your network really is. Oftentimes, individuals when first thinking about this process will respond with, "I don't know anyone." By going through this process, you may be surprised to discover how many people you do, in fact, know reasonably well. Then the process becomes tracking these individuals down so you can reestablish contact. Interestingly, LinkedIn recognizes that people may want to connect again after many years, and it even has in its drop-down menu "getting back in touch." People are recognizing the need to get back in touch, and you should feel empowered to do so, as well. The worst that can happen is that people do not respond. Even if that happens, you have lost nothing.

Building this initial network will give you the impetus to continue to grow and expand the links with people who are in a position to help you professionally. Given that you would like to maintain at least some work–life balance, it is wise to **leave Facebook for your personal life and keep LinkedIn for your professional life**. Remember always the need for mutuality in relationships. When you reach out to someone, make sure you are careful to offer the other person assistance so they can benefit from your skills and network, as well. If you are generous with others, you will help them be generous with you.

Step 3 - Getting Real About the Time this Process Takes

As mentioned above, building this network is a very time-consuming process. One of the key reasons for the previous discussions on finding your core values was to help you consider how to build the necessary support mechanisms you will need so you can stay very positively engaged in what is a very time-consuming process.

A fundamental issue as you go through this process is the challenge that the administration can become potentially overwhelming. Thus, it is important that you explore whatever mechanism works for you, whether that be a spreadsheet to track when and who you contacted, contact management software, or some old-fashioned paper system. The key is that it be something that works for you and that you can continue to work with and retain for a number of years. Particularly for those re-entering the job market, this might be a good reason to brush up your Word, Excel, and PowerPoint skills so you can use those tools to make your life more efficient and bring your skills up to date.

An important part of this system is to deal with most individuals' propensity for procrastination. Finding a mechanism that causes you to spend time researching, writing emails, and following up on the phone, and keeps you doing this day in and day out over the course of many months, will be a critical element in actually achieving your goals and objectives. The reason for thinking of your system as a multiyear capability is that, having made the investment in building a network, you want to find a way to keep track of those in whom you have invested so much.

Recognizing that building and maintaining the network is time consuming and emotionally draining, it is critical to have both an accountability partner to keep you on track and a group to support you. The reality is, if you are to succeed in something as intense as managing your career, you need a personal board of advisors.

In **Team Genius,** Rich Karlgaard and Michael Malone take a detailed look into the new science of teams and the power of different team sizes, from two to seven, to twelve and beyond[32]. Most importantly, they dispel the myth that clever inventions and technological innovations only come from brilliant inventors working by themselves in some lonely log cabin in the North Woods, having some blinding flash of inspiration that proceeded to change the world as we know it. Particularly in Silicon Valley, over the last decade, there has grown the myth of an iconic Steve Jobs as the solo inventor of everything innovative at Apple. What they reveal is that whether it was Thomas Edison, the Lockheed Skunk Works, or Apple, breakthrough technological innovation in the 20th and 21st century is more often the result of inspired teams, rather than some lonely inventor toiling alone in some dark corner.

You need to find the ideal team size that can support you in your quest to create a professional and personal life that has the kind of impact that will leave the kind of legacy that reflects all of your many talents. Again, this will be an iterative process in response to your vision and mission.

Step 4 - Allocating Your Time

As discussed in Chapter 2, if a perfectly executed search takes six months and a **typical self-driven job search process requires 12 to 18 months**, you need to create a system that will keep you on track and keep you going. Implicit within that system is to allocate where you are spending your time. The reality is that approximately **80% of the time will be focused on** going through and **utilizing/growing your network**. As you probably have found from personal experience over the years, the best opportunities are through a referral of referral of a referral, in other words, often at least three steps in the chain. Perhaps 10% of your time can be spent on published positions just to be aware of what the market is doing and what types of positions seem to be available ... and, who knows, you might get lucky.

The final 10% of the time can be allocated to interacting with search firms. Now that you understand some of the nuances of the search process and what goes on behind the curtain, and having discovered that the great and powerful Oz is perhaps not as perfect you believed when you first entered the Emerald

Throne Room, you are now in a position to work more effectively with search firms and how they can become useful allies in your ongoing lifetime career management process.

Each search firm has its own separate universe and cannot work for everyone at the same time for obvious conflict of interest reasons. It is, in fact, one of the challenges of large firms that different parts of the firm in different parts of the country or the world may work for competing firms in a particular industry segment. Naturally, clients are not pleased if a retained search firm poaches their best people to send to another client. So you need to do your homework to determine the correct individuals in the various search firms who are actually doing work in an area and for clients that would be of interest to you.

Summary of Where to Spend Your Time

To summarize, you will have the greatest success finding the opportunities that are interesting to you and meet your needs through people who know and trust you. Therefore, focus your time on building relationships with quality people, including caring for those relationships over time, rather than chasing posted positions and hoping that some search firm will be your pot of gold at the end of the rainbow. Like most things in life, you will get out of this process the energy and care you put into it, remembering always that there is a time lag between sowing and reaping. Consistency will be ultimately rewarded.

Chapter Five

WHY STAYING RELEVANT
MEANS STAYING HEALTHY

Thomas Jefferson's Prescription for Health

HEALTH IS OFTEN REFERRED TO AS ONE OF THOSE things you do not appreciate until you have lost it. History shows that high-performing individuals have always known the importance of health as a critical element to productivity and truly enjoying life. The principal author of the US Declaration of Independence, Thomas Jefferson, noted over two centuries ago, "Leave all the afternoon for exercise and recreation, which are as necessary as reading. I will rather say more necessary because health is worth more than learning[33]." In a similar vein, Jefferson stated, "Not less than two hours a day should be devoted to exercise, and the weather should be little regarded. A person not sick will not be injured by getting wet[34]."

The individual who the U.S. Army called upon at the beginning of World War II to create a fitness program for incoming cadets, Jack LaLanne, often known as the "Godfather of Fitness" echoed Jefferson's sentiment with, "Your health account, your bank account, they're the same thing. The more you put in, the more you can take out. Exercise is king and nutrition is queen. Together you have a kingdom[35]."

The sad facts are that in our in modern first-world society more than two-thirds of the population is overweight or obese and less than 25% achieve the US government's Physical Activity Guideline recommendations of 150 minutes of moderate exercise per week[36]. Lest the reader think that this is a problem only of the middle-aged, the reality is that already in the under-18 age group, Type II diabetes is exceeding 12% in the United States and Western Europe[37]. Ironically, the most economically advanced countries, such as the United States and Germany, have the highest populations with Type II diabetes.

Not surprisingly, there is a close connection between overweight and obesity and Type II diabetes. Ironically, less than a generation ago, Type II diabetes was called "adult onset diabetes" and was something to which only people in their 60s and 70s succumbed[38]. The change in dietary guidelines of the early 80s that allowed sugar to be added at will to the commercial diet while restricting the so-called "bad fat" is now recognized as having played a major part in this societal decline in healthy behavior[39]. The net of all of this change in diet and physical behavior means that this current generation is likely to live not as long as their parents. After several hundred years of continuously increasing life expectancy, our excess consumption, combined with a hyper-sedentary lifestyle, are leading to the natural consequence of reduced quality of life and life expectancy. If you thought the movie *WALL-E* was about sometime far in the future, a casual glance at crowds in most Western cities will show that the future has already arrived[40].

Step 1 - Dealing With the Reality of Western Youth Culture

The reality is that we live in a culture in the Western world that prizes youth, particular body shapes, and accomplishment. If you are 50+ and are trying to keep up with the velocity of change and the typical tempo of corporate life at the senior management level, you need to be perceived as high-energy, dynamic, fit, and able to deal with the stresses of corporate travel. If health issues that are thought to be the result of poor lifestyle choices cause you to be absent from the office on a more than very occasional basis, the ultimate consequence will be a belief in the organization that you are not someone who can be relied upon to be present when needed.

Conversely, if you are seen as someone who models a healthy lifestyle, has the energy to fulfill everything the job throws at you and then some, and because of your endorphins are a very nice person to be around and have a pleasant demeanor, you will continue to be seen as a critical part of the senior management team and someone who is eminently promotable. The Army does not hire people who they consider to have health risks, and many companies have a similar, albeit unwritten, policy. From the company's perspective, it makes sense to invest in motivated individuals who are present and can deliver. So the choice is ultimately up to you, the individual, as to which path you would like to follow to maximize your career opportunities and stay relevant.

What does this mean to you, the 50+ professional? Well, for one thing, if you are not overweight and are achieving the 150-minute physical activity guidelines, you are already in the top 25% of the population! This is also an encouragement for you to maintain a healthy lifestyle that includes plenty of exercise, combined with a well-rounded diet consisting of plenty of fruits and vegetables, combined with normal-sized portions of protein and fat and an avoidance of refined sugars and manufactured products. The easiest way to remember this is to shop along the walls of the grocery store and to avoid the middle aisles at your peril.

Step 2 - How Staying Fit Can Keep You Relevant

The name of an athletic shoe company, ASICS is an acronym derived from the Latin phrase, Anima Sana In Corpore Sano—a sound mind in a sound body[41]. The good news is that creating and keeping a sound body is actually quite doable in today's society. There are a variety of health options to keep you fit. Activities can range from walking at lunchtime, to taking the stairs at work, to joining a company-sponsored team. There are numerous athletic facilities, many of which are open up to 24 hours per day.

One way of achieving this balance and maintaining a healthy exercise routine is to engage in the sport of triathlon. The reasons are quite simple. First, triathlons consist of swimming, biking, and running. These are three disciplines that need to be balanced, something that is a good prescription for life.

Swimming is a lifelong sport that is highly technical and forces the individual to think about body position, balance, core strength, and is sufficiently complex enough that you can always learn something. Given that you can't have a lot of chit chat while you are swimming laps, it is also a great time to focus on breathing, balance, and thinking. Swimming puts you in touch with the very beginnings of your life when you were floating and swimming in the womb of your mother. Because of the discipline involved, swimming teaches breathing and builds aerobic capacity. The real reason you have a brain is to control movement[42]. Because you can never do the same stroke in exactly the same way in a medium as dynamic as water, swimming constantly stimulates new pathways in the nervous system, which helps build a resilient and ever renewing nervous system.

Bicycling, the second part of a triathlon, focuses on smoothness, balance, and freedom. With a bicycle, you can go remarkably long distances efficiently, while still at a pace that allows you to understand and experience your environment. It is a freedom machine and also a transportation mode, such that this is a sport you can incorporate into your daily commute. By cycling to and from work, given the average 16-mile-per-hour speeds of most commutes in the Metro areas of the United States, you are giving up relatively little time compared to driving a car[43]. At the same time, you become intimately aware of the environment between where you live and where you work. This knowledge may well make you more attuned to needs in your community that you might otherwise not be aware of.

Running is the third part of a triathlon and the sport that places the necessary weight bearing on your limbs, keeping at bay your tendency to lose calcium, osteopenia, that is a reality of life after age 30[44]. Running provides the necessary impetus to maintain strong healthy limbs that are resistant to fractures should you have the usual trips and falls that are part of life.

What many people do not realize is that triathlon actually has a fourth discipline, which is nutrition. By engaging in triathlons, you will naturally begin to think about what you eat, when you eat, and portion control. In addition, your knowledge of nutrition will enable you to make healthy choices when you are traveling and confronted by the usual propensity to eat more than you should, consume more alcohol than you should, and not get enough rest.

One of the benefits from being active in triathlon is improved sleep because it teaches you to pay attention to your sleep patterns. This can be very useful if you travel a great deal because it will allow you to more easily and quickly adapt to new time zones if you are the typical professional who travels anywhere from 20 to 40% of the schedule. I say this from experience. I have more than 20 years' experience doing triathlons, including over 13 years doing Ironman triathlons, all while traveling over 2 million air miles during that time. Triathlons keep your life in balance.

Step 3 - How Triathlon Can Help You Build High-Performance Management Teams

With respect to building and maintaining high performing teams, triathlons also have a number of useful features. Triathlons come in many shapes and sizes. You start with the simplest Sprint distance, 500 meters swimming, 20 km bicycling, and 5 km run. You can then progress to the Olympic distance, which is approximately 1,500 meter swim, 40 km bike, and 10 km run. Moving up to the so-called 70.3 or Half Ironman involves distances of 1,900 meter swim, 90 km bike, and a half marathon of 21.1 km. The full Ironman is just the usual 2.4 miles or 3,800 meters of swimming, followed by 112 miles or 180 km on the bike, and then a simple marathon of 26.2 miles or 42.2 km as the conclusion. When you add up the distances, an Ironman is 140.6 miles for the day. The great thing about Ironman is that you don't have to worry about getting warmed up for the run.

With respect to building high-performance teams, triathlons can build collegiality because most events can be done as a relay team. This means that individuals can participate in achieving a common goal, with each team member doing the sport in which they feel most comfortable. Over time, they can explore the other disciplines, again as part of the team. As a broader group, the sharing of experiences, including tips on how to incorporate physical activity and healthy nutrition as part of a lifestyle, allows for increased opportunities for team members to share with one another. While different events have different challenges, there is nothing like being able to walk in on Monday morning and tell your coworkers that you've just completed a triathlon.

With the variety of distances and disciplines, triathlons allow Type A personalities to have events on which they can build, burn off the normal stress of work, and have enough endorphins to remain pleasant and motivating people. For those less driven or who are part of a team, the shorter distances still allow a sense of accomplishment in keeping with their personality.

With respect to the biomechanics of the sport, a triathlon involves moving in straight lines without having other people bang into you. You won't twist your ankle sliding into third base in a triathlon. This allows for people who may not do as well at team sports to nevertheless feel a part of the team and be able to identify with the discussions in the break room that so often revolve around sports and activities.

The beauty of triathlon in the modern world is that there is sufficient technology to support those individuals who may feel uncomfortable in either swimming, cycling, or running to obtain specialized instruction, often with video analysis, which allows the thoughtful professional to make great strides in a short time so they are comfortable, confident, and can enjoy themselves. For example, the typical corporate weekend retreat, generally billed under the term of "team building" and which sometimes for the more adventurous includes a ropes course or whitewater rafting, could easily be converted into a triathlon clinic, where by the end of the weekend, individuals have completed, perhaps as a team, their first sprint triathlon. The endorphins that flow as a result of an accomplishment like this, particularly for those who may have felt at the beginning of the weekend less than comfortable in classic sports that involve significant hand-eye coordination, such as softball, basketball, or other team sports, provide a sense of accomplishment in the sports arena that allows them to have equal bragging rights when they come to work on Monday morning.

Summary of Staying Relevant by Staying Healthy

Work in the modern super inter-connected world still can be very physically, mentally, and emotionally demanding. The global economy requires varying levels of travel, stress, and sleep deprivation if you want to stay close to your far flung web of suppliers and customers. The bottom line is that if you want to stay relevant at 50+ in modern corporate life, you need to incorporate the wisdom of Thomas Jefferson into your lifestyle so you can flawlessly execute the physical demands of your professional life, all while making it look very easy.

Chapter Six

WHY PAYING IT FORWARD IS YOUR BEST CAREER INSURANCE POLICY

Paying It Forward Just Makes Good Sense

HAVING MADE IT THIS FAR, WITH THE WISDOM THAT COMES from having experienced much of life, you now understand why you need to plan the next 30+ years, why you rarely get a call back from the search firm, how to create and implement a strategic career plan that will position you with a portfolio of opportunities to stay in the best possible position at all times, and you have a program to stay physically fit so you can stay mentally fit and professionally relevant. In a sense, you have made it. However, thinking about the long term, as you now do, also spare some thought for how you got here and how you define success. As the old African Proverb quite simply states, "**If you want to go fast, go alone. If you want to go far, go together**." Your success is a direct reflection of the helping hands you have received from others along the way. So what is your obligation to the universe?

Pay it forward. If you are honest with yourself, many people have given freely to you over the years and received no direct compensation for it. Paying it forward means the way you repay the kindness you received from others is to extend the same kindness to others. Think about your legacy, think about David Brooks' eulogy virtues, and think about how you can make a difference every day. In this process, recall the times when you were struggling and did not know where your next opportunity was going to come from, and someone reached out to you or responded to your overtures and helped you along the way. Similarly, your societal responsibility is to look for opportunities to help others. When others need help, that is your opportunity to promote the common good and do unto others as you would like to have done unto you.

As humans, we cheer for our heroes, but we connect with them on a personal level in those moments when they are at their point of greatest adversity. Superman becomes real when he struggles with an evil enemy trying to kill him with kryptonite. Mr. Incredible is most lovable when he realizes that he is overweight and needs to go on an exercise and weight loss program. As you struggle with the world that has or is treating you "unfairly," you, too, can relate to, and extend a helping hand to, those who are facing similar adversities. See in your challenges and defeats the opportunities to help others and find true happiness as depicted by Thomas Jefferson, John Adams, and Benjamin Franklin. As you do something for others, you will grow profoundly within yourself and find ways to identify and create a true sense of centeredness and gratitude.

The Real Pursuit of Happiness

Looking back at history, we can see what the pursuit of happiness really meant. When Thomas Jefferson used that phrase in the Declaration of Independence, he was not thinking of some narcissistic pursuit of individual pleasure. Rather, he was thinking of the freedom of opportunity to be able to pursue those endeavors that would improve the well-being of society as a whole. In his 2005 lecture at the National Conference on Citizenship, US Supreme Court Justice Anthony Kennedy expressed his concern that while in modern times there is a "hedonistic component" to the definition of *happiness*, in contrast for the framers of the Declaration of Independence, "Happiness meant that feeling of self-worth and dignity you acquire by contributing to your community and to its civic life." In the context of the Declaration of Independence, *happiness* was about an individual's contribution to society, rather than pursuits of self-gratification. **The pursuit of happiness is really about paying it forward for the benefit of all, rather than grasping for it all only for yourself.**

One of the benefits of being 50+ is that you have come to realize that life is a process, a journey, and a flow, not a destination. When you were younger, you may have thought of life as a series of destinations: graduating from high school, graduating from college, getting your first job, etc. With time, you have come to realize that there are, in fact, cycles in your life and the lives of those around you. Those cycles sometimes go up and sometimes go down. Life flows like the rise and fall of the tides.

Integrity is the Basis for a Consistent Harvest

As you think about these cycles, they are much like the seasons in the year. After the bleakness of the winter, spring begins and the ground opens up and becomes ready for seeds to be planted. Once planted, the ground needs to be watered, weeds removed, and some fertilizer never hurts the process. In time, the shoots grow and the crop ripens and becomes ready for the harvest. If you have done the process correctly, the harvest will be excellent. On the other hand, if you have shortchanged the process and cut corners, the harvest is often poor.

So, too, in your life you will have times of planting, times of nurturing, and times of harvesting. As Rick Warren is fond of saying, "There's always a delay between sowing and reaping. You plant in one season, and you harvest in another[45]." If you try to plant and harvest at the same time, you will only dig up the seeds that you just planted.

This process is the same in your professional life. If you do the right thing, have integrity, and remain consistent and positive in your approach to life, your work, and others, at the appropriate season, you will be able to harvest. If you help others, at some point others will help you. If you never help others, it is unlikely that they will help you. So it is that paying it forward is an excellent insurance policy against the likely chance that things will not always go perfectly. From time to time, you will need the help of others, so it is wise to have invested in the cosmic bank of good deeds so you will have something to draw on when things are not going so well.

Being Strong by Sharing Your Weakness

One very personal way of paying it forward is to recognize that people are most effective at connecting with others when they share their pain or weakness. In sharing that pain, you become real to those around you and are able to speak with an authority on that point that no one else can. If you have gone through the pain of being fired, laid off, or rejected at finding work, then to others who are in a similar situation, you have the ability to speak a word of hope that no one else can. As a mentor who walks alongside someone else, you possess an authority that is unique to you and based on your own personal journey.

As an experienced professional, you have learned much in the process called life. You have had frustrations, setbacks, and defeats. Things have not always worked out the way you wanted. However, you have also learned skills that have allowed you to overcome those obstacles and make lemonade out of lemons. This learning can be put to the benefit of others by paying it forward and helping them. In doing so, you leave a legacy that, like the butterfly effect, allows your wings of wisdom to multiply into a hurricane of positive energy throughout the world. That is your challenge and your opportunity for the rest of your life. **Carpe diem**. **Seize it.**

1. https://en.wikipedia.org/wiki/Joe_Friday

2. http://www.ssa.gov/planners/life expectancy.html

3. http://www.fool.com/retirement/general/ 2012/10/15/17-frightening-facts-about-retirement-savings-in-.aspx

4. http://money.cnn.com/2015/01/29/ retirement/401k-balances/

5. www.ssa.gov/planners/lifeexpectancy.html

6. U.S. Census Bureau, P23-212,65+ in the United States: 2010, U.S. Government Printing Office, Washington, DC,2014, page 5

7. U.S. Census Bureau, P23-212,65+ in the United States: 2010, U.S. Government Printing Office, Washington, DC,2014, page 5

8. U.S. Census Bureau, P23-212,65+ in the United States: 2010, U.S. Government Printing Office, Washington, DC,2014, page 5

9. U.S. Census Bureau, P23-212,65+ in the United States: 2010, U.S. Government Printing Office, Washington, DC,2014, pages 10- 11

10. http://www.fool.com/retirement/general /2015/01/10/the-typical-american-has-this-much-in-retirement-s.aspx

11. http://www.coveredca.com

12. http://www.businessinsider.com/health-care-costs-will-exceed-average-household-income-by-2030-2012-3

13. Fisher, Kenneth L. and Lara Hoffmans, Plan Your Prosperity: the only retirement guide you'll ever need, starting now, whether you are 22, 52 or 82(Hoboken: John Wiley & Sons, 2013)

14. Fisher and Hoffmans, 59-72.

15. Fisher and Hoffmans, 72.

16. Pink, Daniel H., Free Agent Nation: How America's New Independent Workers Are Transforming the Way We Live)New York, Warner Books, 2001)

17. 2014 North American Staffing and Recruiting Trends Report, Bullhorn, Inc.

18. Brooks, David, The Moral Bucket List, April 21, 2015, NYTimes, http://www.nytimes.com/2015/04/12/opinion/sunday/david-brooks-the-moral-bucket-list.html?_r=0

19. Keirsey, David and Marilyn Bates, Please Understand Me (Del Mar, Prometheus Nemesis Book Company, 1978)

20. https://en.wikipedia.org/wiki/Johari_window

21. Shakespeare, William, Julius Caesar (Act I, Scene 2, L. 140-141)

22. Sharone, Ofer, Flawed System/Flawed Self: Job Searching and Unemployment Experiences(Chicago, University of Chicago Press,2013)

23. https://en.wikipedia.org/wiki/First_ inauguration_of_Franklin_D._Roosevelt

24. http://www.nytimes.com/2015/04/ 12/opinion/sunday/david-brooks-the-moral-bucket-list.html?_r=0

25. http://www.nytimes.com/2015/04/ 12/opinion/sunday/david-brooks-the-moral-bucket-list.html?_r=0

26. Desiderata, https://en.wikipedia.org/wiki/ Desiderata

27. Ortberg, John, When the Game is Over, It all goes back in the box(Grand Rapids, Zondervan, 2007)

28. https://en.wikipedia.org/wiki/Where_ no_man_has_gone_before

29. Life 2.0; How People Across America are Transforming Their Lives by Finding the Where of Their Happiness(New York, Crown Business, 2004)

30. https://en.wikipedia.org/wiki/The_Great_ Waldo_Pepper

31. http://www.imdb.com/title/tt0145487/

quotes; Luke 12:48

32. Karlgaard, Rich and Michael S. Malone, Team Genius: The New Science of High Performing Organizations(New York, HarperCollins, 2015)

33. https://www.monticello.org/site/research-and-collections/exercise

34. https://www.monticello.org/site/research-and-collections/exercise

35. https://en.wikipedia.org/wiki/Jack_LaLanne

36. http://www.cdc.gov/physicalactivity/basics/adults/

37. International Diabetes Foundation Report, Sixth Edition, 2013, http://www.allcountries.org/ranks/diabetes_prevalence_country_ranks.html

38. http://www.mayoclinic.org/diseases-conditions/type-2-diabetes/basics/definition/con-20031902

39. https://en.wikipedia.org/wiki/Robert_Lustig

40. http://www.imdb.com/title/tt0910970/

41. http://www.asicsamerica.com/about-asics

42. http://www.ted.com/talks/daniel_wolpert_the_real_reason_for_brains?language=en

43. https://smartasset.com/mortgage/what-will-my-commute-be

44. http://www.webmd.com/osteoporosis/tc/osteopenia-overview

45. http://rickwarren.org/devotional/english/plant-today-then-be-patient-for-the-harvest